God in the Age of Science

Shane Andre

Copyright © 2021 Shane Andre
Copyright © 2021 Generis Publishing

All rights reserved. This book or any portion thereof may not be reproduced or used in any manner whatsoever without the written permission of the publisher except for the use of brief quotations in a book review.

Title: God in the Age of Science

ISBN: 978-1-63902-781-1

Author: Shane Andre

Cover image: www.pixabay.com

Publisher: Generis Publishing
Online orders: www.generis-publishing.com
Contact email: info@generis-publishing.com

To Lea, who gave me birth and shape;
to Suzanne, who put up with my quirks for over fifty years;
and to Lee and his family,
who face the future beyond our ken.

TABLE OF CONTENTS

INTRODUCTION 9

THE PROBLEM OF EVIL AND THE PARADOX OF FRIENDLY ATHEISM 21

WAS HUME AN ATHEIST? 35

ARE WE DESCARTES' BABIES? 67

CAN NATURALISM ALLOW FOR EVIL? 83

SCIENCE AND RELIGION: AN ALTERNATIVE VIEW OF AN ANCIENT RIVALRY 105

THE PROBLEM WITH THE PROBLEM OF EVIL 129

SHANE ANDRE: BRIEF AUTOBIOGRAPHY 159

INTRODUCTION

As a child in Montreal, I was exposed to three major religious influences--Protestantism, Catholicism, and Theosophy—that may help to explain the origin of my thoughts about religion. The first came about through Quebec's division of public education into Protestant schools (usually Anglophone) and Catholic schools (usually Francophone). Though a Francophone school was on my street within a half block, I walked several blocks away (about half a mile) to attend Strathcona, the nearest grade school for English-speaking children. There we began each day by singing "God Save the King" (this was World War II) and listening to a short passage from the King James Bible, read aloud by our classroom teacher as we followed it with our open Bibles. Whatever it was, I absorbed it without protest or curiosity, as if it were part of the scenery.

The only interruption in this sequence was the year I spent in a Catholic boarding school, when my mother suffered an extended illness and was unable to provide care. Religion now became obvious, not just because we children were surrounded by nuns, but because we were taught special prayers, said grace before meals, attended church two or three times a week, confessed our sins, and were prepared for confirmation. Young boys had to wear shorts when bathed by a nun. Religion was taken very seriously by Catholic educators, but so were the three R's. Thanks to the basic skills my teachers developed, I was able to skip grade two and go directly to grade three when I returned to public school the following year.

Theosophy was another story. Impressed by the good works of Brother Andre, my mother had a brief flirtation with Catholicism. It was probably in this period she changed her name to "Lea Andre." (She said later she admired the saint and wanted a first name that couldn't be shortened.) But the flirtation didn't last long. Looking for something less doctrinaire, Lea turned to Theosophy and became a life-long member of that sect. She accepted the doctrine of karma and reincarnation because, she said, that was the only way life could be fair. How else explain the fact that, while some children were born to loving and caring parents, many others were not?

Lea did not try to impose her newfound beliefs on me, but encouraged me to think for myself and to express my own point of view. Though even as a youngster I was skeptical about reincarnation—after all, I had no memory of a previous life—I had nothing better to fall back upon than renewals of doubt.

Nevertheless, at monthly meetings of the Theosophical Society downtown, the members were especially nice to me (usually, I was the only child there). They encouraged me to enjoy the pastries and goodies that were passing around, and so I came to look forward to those meetings—meetings that demanded no commitment. Though I had no idea what truth was, I found it easy to accept broadsides like "There is no religion higher than truth." Years later, as a young man, I even read Madame Blavatsky's massive work, The Secret Doctrine, cover to cover. Now, as an old man, I wish she had kept the secret to herself.

I learned early on that some beliefs are so deeply entrenched that they resist change, and further that they can vary from person to person. For example, my mother believed throughout her life that life had to be fair, whatever accommodation that required of other beliefs. On the other hand, I found it easy to believe that life was not fair, and had little time for the beliefs, religious or otherwise, that life-is-fair required. No doubt I have my own stock of deep-seated, almost irresistible beliefs, such as "Truth is independent of belief." When opposed by anti-realists or post-modern relativists, I prefer to dig in and challenge the challengers rather than to seriously reconsider my fixed positions.

John Hick, the British-American philosopher, said the world in religiously ambiguous, open to more than one interpretation. Despite its dark side, it can be seen in a religious light, as he so well demonstrated. At the same time, despite intervals of brightness, it can easily be seen as a vale of tribulation, where sacrifice is demanded, suffering is unavoidable, and hopes are often crushed. I have struggled with these different perspectives most of my life. Responding to the beauty of nature and the glory of music, it is easy to believe that the world is greater than we know; but, equally, when it comes to "man's inhumanity to man" and the waste and ugliness we impose upon nature, the world appears to be no more than a boneyard. To ask what it "really" is, is to ask a question to which, in my opinion, no objective answer is available. You see what you are looking for, and if you are looking for delight and wonder, or fearful of distress and disappointment, the world will cooperate: you will see no end of it.

I know of no way to bring these two perspectives together other than to see them as variable aspects of a world which, in itself, is neither delightful nor terrible. It is a world which provides the opportunity to exercise our values, but otherwise is indifferent to them. The world isn't on our side or against us. It doesn't have to take sides, and it doesn't. It provides the theater but not the script. The script is what people write, and they write it in a variety of ways, to which "the house" has its own responses. To paraphrase an old saying: man proposes; the house disposes.

Admittedly, this view is familiar; in fact, for those who believe it, it is a platitude. It is a platitude because some form of it has appealed to many thinkers, from Epicurus and Lucretius to Hume and Bertrand Russell, and beyond. Where metaphysics is concerned, I think of it today as a form of scientific naturalism; where epistemology goes, as a form of pragmatic empiricism; and where ethics goes, perhaps as the form of the non-descriptivism and rule-utilitarianism advocated by R. M. Hare. I am aware that all of these views are controversial;

there is no public or professional consensus for any of them, which suggests to me that they aren't really platitudes. If they are platitudes, it is only because they express a point of view which is known universally, not because it is universally accepted.

This is not the place to try to defend scientific naturalism, or pragmatic empiricism, or rule-utilitarianism. Instead, I will take them for granted and explore a set of more specific, but germane, issues: Is theism true and rational to believe? What did Hume think of "natural religion"? Why is belief in metaphysical dualism both natural and yet preposterous? Can naturalism allow for evil or only for bad people? Are science and religion incompatible? Is the existence of evil evidence against the existence of God? Let me add a few words about the articles that follow.

"The Problem of Evil and the Paradox of Friendly Atheism" took off from an NEH Summer Research Seminar in 1981 at Purdue University on "Truth and Rationality in Theistic Belief," conducted by William Rowe. Enthusiastic as I was about the concept of friendly atheism, I concluded that its argument for atheism, based on the Bambi example, failed to close the gap between the appearance of pointless suffering (which nobody denies) and the reality of pointless suffering (which theists generally deny). On the other hand, I thought that his "friendly" form of atheism was welcome and correct: regardless of whether theism was true or false, theistic belief could be rationally justified. So, of course, could atheistic belief. Rational methods of inquiry were powerless to resolve certain questions.

Prof. Rowe was not perturbed by my conclusion, for his position had already been challenged by others. He thrust a paper by Delmar Lewis into my hand, "The Problem with the Problem of Evil," which contended that Rowe's argument for atheism was marred by an "inductive slide." Rowe attempted to respond to such criticisms by revising his case in subsequent papers, but, as I argue in my own version of "The Problem with the Problem of Evil," he never succeeded in closing the gap.

My article on Hume grew out of another NEH Summer Research Seminar, "Church, State, and Moral Control in Early Modern Europe," at Northwestern University, 1990, under the direction of William E. Monter. My target was the widespread belief that David Hume, the greatest philosopher of the eighteenth century writing in English, was an atheist. Though I had shared this belief early in my career, I modified it on reading his work more extensively. Both his *Natural History of Religion* and *Dialogues Concerning Natural Religion* convinced me that, though Hume was opposed to traditional Christian theism, neither was he prepared to go the other extreme, the atheism of the French *philosophes* of the period. His conclusion, as I interpret it, could be put in this guarded form: monotheism might be true, but if it were, it would be in the form of a God who was limited in power or goodness. Christians, of course, had no time for a finite God, and so many of them saw no difference between Hume's position and atheism. Had Hume lived another hundred years, into the time of Darwin, he might well have revised his qualified support for theism.

In "Are We Descartes Babies?" I take on the task of examining metaphysical dualism—the worldview that envisages reality in terms of two worlds, as expressed in Plato's world of changing appearances and the ideal world of unchanging forms, Descartes' world of extended things and the world of conscious minds, and Kant's division between the world of subjective phenomena and the world of objective noumena. Not so well-known but no less dualistic are the worldviews of monotheistic religion, whether Christian, Judaic, or Islamic. There is the primary world, inhabited by God and possibly other supernatural beings like angels and demons, and the secondary world, occupied by created things, like water and rocks, plants and animals. As embodied souls, humans have a foot (so to speak) in both domains. Their souls, immaterial and immortal, belong to the primary domain; their bodies, material and perishable, to the secondary domain. While these images give us some idea of metaphysical dualism, it would be a mistake to associate them exclusively with philosophy or religion, for, according to psychologist Paul Bloom, humans are "natural dualists." They find it easy to think of themselves as one kind of thing—something that matters--and of other things (including sometimes, other humans) as another kind of thing--something that doesn't matter as much. Humans can think, not just of what they perceive, but of what they can't perceive at the moment, and by thinking of it gain some control over it, giving them a sense of supernatural freedom. You can do things with your mind--recall the past, anticipate the future, imagine counterfactual scenarios--that you can't do with your body, so it is easy to imagine that you are both a mind and a body.

Thinking along these lines, I wanted to investigate the ideas that might lead us, apart from religion or philosophy, to be natural dualists. I came up with four ideas, each of which seemed to have some intuitive plausibility, but none of which seemed to bear critical examination. My critique of dualistic worldviews may be regarded as so many riffs on Bloom's big idea of natural dualism. I believe he approved of it, if not in detail, at least in principle. As I see it, dualism has its roots in the fact that man is an animal who aspires to be more than an animal. We can glory in that aspiration, as it leads to all the good things that distinguish us, at least in degree, from other animals—language, science, technology, the fine arts, rationality, and morality—but we should never forget that we share the planet with other animals. Just as we speak of "whales and other mammals," not of "whales and mammals," we should speak of "humans and other animals," not of "humans and animals."

My paper "Can Naturalism Allow for Evil?" was too ambitious for its own good. In it I sought to do something that could not be done properly short of a book, so it turned out to be little more than a program for future work. It undertook to compare the metaphysics, epistemology, and ethical systems of two giant and variable worldviews, theism and naturalism, and to argue for the modest superiority of the latter. Taking suffering as the root of badness and evil as the extreme form of badness, I took over the theological distinction between moral and natural evil and suggested how it could be used by naturalists to show that some human actions, whether intentional or not, were genuinely evil. I thought that outcome answered my title question, but many of my colleagues thought otherwise. Nevertheless, none of their objections, I recall, showed that my explanations of the meaning of my two key terms were faulty, or that they failed to support my affirmative conclusion. I take this as evidence, not that my thesis is correct, but that, despite the objections, it was not refuted. However, my critics were absolutely right in suggesting that much more work needed to be done. Sadly, I have never been able to complete that task, and I have no hope of completing it now. I do hope, however, that the other papers included in this collection will fill one or two blanks.

My article "Science and Religion: An Alternative View of an Ancient Rivalry" took aim at the popular belief that the two magisteria, as Stephen Jay Gould called them, are in conflict. I argued, on the contrary, that there is a difference between "religion" and "a religion," and that while the latter might favor the creation story over the theory of evolution, there was no call for the former to do so. I drew a number of analogies between the "family of religions" and the "family of sciences," but, regretfully, failed to note some commonalities between the two families: both entertain worldviews about the place of humans in the world, both regard the achievement of information about the world as challenging but possible, and both consider the good life for man as attainable but not guaranteed.

Despite these analogies, there are important disanalogies between the two families. I note three such differences: whereas the family of sciences is coherent, unified by a common method, but not centrally concerned with moral guidance, the family of religions is virtually the opposite. Taken as a collective, it is neither coherent nor unified by a common method, and unlike the sciences it is centrally concerned with moral guidance. Matthew Arnold even goes so far as to say that religion is morality tinged by emotion, and Stephen Jay Gould regards religion, not science or philosophy, as the magisterium concerned with the meaning of life, values, and morality. Taking for granted the fact/value dichotomy, Gould proposes that the magisterium of science is concerned with other matters-- the discovery of facts and laws of nature—and his NOMA-principle insists on the independence of the two domains.

While I have reservations about Gould's proposal, I support his view that science is not in the morality business, at least in the way exemplified by religion. Nevertheless, two qualifications are necessary. First, as the sad history of Social Darwinism and the eugenics movement shows, moralists have often coopted science to push their social agendas. Second, as everyone knows, there is a close connection between science and technology. Roughly, science provides information that can then be used to improve human life by the invention of new technologies. As the advertisement for Dow Chemical Company put it, "Better living through chemistry." Viewed in this light, science can be seen as the benefactor of mankind, but that is only a half-truth. The other half of the truth is that, since human interests are often in conflict, science and technology in a commercial marketplace are, like a prostitute, available to the highest bidder. The nuclear bombs that Americans build to protect themselves from Russian or Chinese surprise attack are rightly seen by them as a Damocles sword held over their heads. No, big science isn't for sale, but scientists are, and they are well-paid to serve their national interests, even if those conflicting interests might lead to the end of the world as we know it. In a civilization dominated by commercial interests, the celebrated neutrality of science is only a fig-leaf to cover an ugly truth. If anything is clear, it is that science is different from the use of science, and it may be impossible to separate them.

My final essay, "The Problem with the Problem of Evil," briefly reviews the history of the problem and examines the controversy between two of its leading spokesmen, William Rowe and Alvin Plantinga. Despite their pointed disagreement about the existence of pointless suffering and God, both seem to take for granted the same grand idea: pointless suffering is suffering that God could not prevent without thereby losing a greater good or permitting an evil equally bad or worse. While Rowe proposes that there are cases of pointless suffering, so defined, Plantinga responds that, for all we know, God may have a morally sufficient reason for permitting such evils. At this point the disagreement appears to be intractable. Who knows whether God exists, or, if "he" does, whether he has a morally sufficient reason for permitting what would otherwise be horrendous evils? I don't, and in my opinion neither do Rowe nor Plantinga.

My response to the stalemate is to bracket the metaphysical question about God and his reasons, and to return to earthbound conceptions of pointless suffering. Many things have been said about suffering, but I think most people would agree that intense and protracted suffering, whether physical like a burn or psychological like grief, is bad for the one who suffers. Call it Suffering with a capital S. Under what conditions would it make sense to call Suffering "pointless"? Well, if the sufferer had done something very bad, like raping a child, some people would say that he deserved it, so his Suffering in prison has a point, if only by protecting the public. Or, to consider another kind of case, think of Job, who was innocent of wrong-doing but underwent great Suffering without cursing his maker, and who eventually was rewarded for his faithfulness by gaining twice as much as he lost. Wouldn't we hesitate to say that his Suffering was pointless? Reflecting on such cases led me to the tentative conclusion that Suffering is pointless if it is neither deserved nor likely to benefit the patient. While it would be awful to have a limb amputated, it would not be pointless if that was the only way to save the patient's life.

While there may be other ways of explaining the concept, I contend only that there are ordinary ways of understanding the concept of pointless suffering that make sense and do not require speculation about God and his reasons. Given such a concept, I expect that we will find that some cases of Suffering are indeed pointless, that other cases of Suffering are not, and that still other cases of Suffering are too complicated for easy call.

The point of this exercise, of course, is not to prove or disprove the existence of God. I suggest that, if our resources are limited, as they usually are, the point of identifying some cases of Suffering as pointless is to give them priority of treatment. For example, when it comes to medical care, it seems appropriate to give priority of care to those patients who Suffer pointlessly. Similarly, if rationing of social goods is required because there is not enough to go around, it seems fair to give individuals who Suffer pointlessly first call upon the needed goods. While no single principle of morality is likely to satisfy the requirements of morality, surely the principle of relieving suffering should be given high priority, especially when Suffering is neither deserved nor of benefit to the one who suffers.

The six articles collected here were written between 1983 and 2021, four of which were published before. I hereby gratefully acknowledge permission to reprint "The Problem of Evil and the Paradox of Friendly Atheism" from the International Journal for Philosophy of Religion, to the journal Hume Studies for permission to reprint "Was Hume an Atheist?" and to the Open Journal of

Philosophy for permission to reprint the two articles "Science and Religion: An Alternative View of an Ancient Rivalry" and "The Problem with the Problem of Evil."

The remaining two articles "Are We Descartes' Babies?" and "Can Naturalism Allow for Evil?" were never submitted for publication. I sent a copy of the first to Prof. Paul Bloom for comment, to which he wrote a brief reply, indicating that he had no objection to the views expressed and looked forward to news of its publication. I sent a copy of the second to Prof. Rowe for comment, to which he replied with appreciation but without critical comment beyond saying that he had learned something from it. I also shared the paper with a group of colleagues organized by Prof. Jerry Manheim. To my surprise and dismay, it provoked a blizzard of negative comment from thinkers who, I thought, largely shared my naturalistic outlook. Disappointed by its reception, I stuck it in my files. Despite its limitations, however, I still think it represents my thinking on one of the toughest problems for naturalism—ethics. If it encourages other thinkers to take the next step forward, it will have served its purpose.

Finally, I am grateful to my editor, Anna Rothman, for both suggesting this project and helping me to see it through.

Nanaimo, British Columbia, 2021

THE PROBLEM OF EVIL AND THE PARADOX OF FRIENDLY ATHEISM

From ancient times philosophers and theologians have debated the significance of suffering and other forms of evil for the belief that the world is the creation of a wholly good, omniscient, and omnipotent being — God. Briefly, two major positions on this question are possible: (1) that God and evil are incompatible, forcing us to reject either theism or the reality of evil[1]; and (2) that God and evil are not incompatible, allowing the theist to recognize, while having to explain, the reality of evil[2]. Historically, atheists have tended to support the first position and theists the second, but, in an important article "The Problem of Evil and Some Varities of Atheism,"[3] William L. Rowe argues for the possibility of a form of atheism ("friendly atheism") which recognizes the logical compatibility of God and evil but holds that the great amount and variety of human and animal suffering makes it reasonable to be an atheist, though it neither disproves theism *nor does it require the atheist to regard the theist as being irrational.*

While this possibility marks a distinct advance over traditional atheism, especially in its distinction between the truth and rationality of theistic belief, I believe that it is liable to certain difficulties which, as far as I know, have not hitherto been noted. After a brief summary of Rowe's position, as I understand it, I propose to argue that two forms of friendly atheism can be distinguished: (1) special grounds atheism, which allows for the rationality of theism but holds that the evidential position of the theist is, in some respects, inferior to that of the atheist; and (2) paradoxical atheism, which allows for the rationality of theism without holding that the atheist knows anything which the theist does not. I hope to show that neither of these positions is acceptable as it stands: the former because it is not new and remains as controversial as ever; and the latter because it is not just paradoxical but incoherent. I conclude that friendly atheism, for all its contribution to the discussion of the rationality of theism, is a contentious concept whose value has yet to be demonstrated.

Rowe crisply states the "argument for atheism based on evil" as follows:

1. There exist instances of intense suffering which an omnipotent, omniscient being could have prevented without thereby losing some greater good or permitting some evil equally bad or worse.

2. An omniscient, wholly good being would prevent the occurrence of any intense suffering it could, unless it could not do so without thereby losing some greater good or permitting some evil equally bad or worse.

3. There does not exist an omnipotent, omniscient, wholly goodbeing.[4]

Since the argument is valid, the question whether it proves its conclusion turns upon the question whether we know its premises to be true. And since the second premise can be regarded as a necessary truth, expressing part of the concept of a theistic God, the crux of the argument reduces to premise (1). Rowe undertakes to motivate us to accept this premise by instancing the case of the suffering fawn. A distant forest fire started by lightning (not human free will) traps and horribly burns a fawn (a creature, we may suppose, which is morally 'Innocent" but capable of experiencing intense suffering), which lingers in pain for several days before it dies. The fawn example illustrates what hardly anyone would care to deny: that there certainly *appear* to be cases of pointless suffering or gratuitous evil in the world. It doesn't follow, of course, that such cases *are* what they *appear* to be. For this reason, Rowe admits that cases like the suffering fawn do not prove that (1) is true.

Nevertheless, such cases make it reasonable to believe that (1) is true. The reason is that, while this or that particular case of apparently pointless suffering might be morally justified by reasons of which we are at present ignorant, the great amount and variety of human and animal suffering make it extremely unlikely that this should turn out to be true of *all* such cases. Supposedly, the atheist is justified in concluding that his basic argument, while it fails as a proof, nevertheless succeeds as a probabilistic argument.

Rowe is aware that the theist is not without a number of replies, of which the strongest, he proposes, is the following inversion of the atheist's basic argument:

3'. There exists an omnipotent, omniscient, wholly good being.

2'. An omniscient, wholly good being would prevent the occurrence of any intense suffering it could, unless it could not do so without thereby losing some greater good or permitting some evil equally bad or worse.

1'. It is not the case that there exist instances of intense suffering which an omnipotent, omniscient being could have prevented without thereby losing some greater good or permitting some evil quality bad or worse.

Like the atheist's argument, this argument is valid and its acceptability hinges upon its first premise, which, of course, is the negation of the conclusion of the original argument. The theist is also like the atheist in that he can cite reasons for accepting the critical premise of his argument: one or more of the traditional arguments for the existence of God, the appeal to religious experience, or the use of theism as an explanatory hypothesis. The acid question is whether any of these reasons is adequate to justify premise (3'), but Rowe does not attempt to evaluate them, as he does the atheist's reasons.[5] Instead, he shifts the question to what might be the atheist's best response to the theist.

Of course, the atheist regards the theist as having a false belief, but what position should the atheist take concerning the *rationality* of the theist's belief?

Rowe distinguishes three major positions on this question and argues in favor of the third. First, the atheist may believe that no one is rationally justified in believing in theism (unfriendly atheism). Second, the atheist may hold no belief concerning the rationality of theism (indifferent atheism). Third, the atheist may believe that some theists are rationally justified in believing in theism (friendly atheism). Rowe's argument for friendly atheism consists of two parts. In the first, he argues that, since it is possible to be rationally justified in believing something which in fact is false, the atheist is not committed to regarding theism as irrational. A terrorist planting a bomb on an airplane may believe both that no one will leave the plane alive and that its passengers are rationally justified in believing otherwise (my example). In this case, of course, the terrorist knows something which the passengers don't, and so the possibility of his position is easily understood. But if person A has more or less the same evidence as person B, is it possible for A to believe both that not-p and that B is rationally justified in believing that p?

This is where the second part of Rowe's argument for friendly atheism comes in. While admitting that friendly atheism can become paradoxical "when the atheist contemplates believing that the theist has all the grounds for atheism that he, the atheist, has, and yet is rationally justified in maintaining his theistic belief," Rowe offers an ingenious example to resolve the paradox.[6] Suppose that I add a long list of numbers three times and get the same result x each time. I inform you of all of this, and so "you have pretty much the same evidence I have" for believing that the sum is x. However, you then tote up the numbers twice on your calculator and arrive at result y, leading you to believe that the sum is not x. What you don't know is that your calculator has been damaged and is therefore unreliable; were you to know this, you would not be justified in believing what you do, but since you don't know this, you are justified. Since I know that your calculator has been damaged, I can believe all these things: (1) that the sum is x; (2) that you have access to my evidence for believing that the sum is x; and (3) that nevertheless you are rationally justified in believing otherwise. This combination of conditions is possible because I have some reason to think that your grounds are not as telling as you take them to be. And if this possibility exists in the general case, why shouldn't it exist in the atheist's case?

It must be admitted that the concept of friendly atheism is appealing. It allows the atheist to maintain the core of his position, that there is no theistic God, without having to maintain the irrationality of theism. Since many theists, even today, are eminent philosophers, whose claim to rationality in matters of religion would be challenged only as a last resort, this concession to theism is in the interest of the atheist. The theist, too, is likely to welcome the concept of friendly atheism, for, while it does not grant him as much as he wishes, he may regard it as a stepping stone to accepting theism. While there is still a gap between a rational and a true belief, it is tempting to think that a rational belief is more likely to be true than is an irrational belief. Hence, the rationality of a belief counts for something even where truth is the prime concern.

Despite these attractions, however, I believe that friendly atheism is much more problematic than at first appears to be the case. Implicit in Rowe's account is a distinction between two forms of this position, which I will call special grounds atheism and paradoxical atheism, or SGA and PA for short. While both are "friendly" to the theist, they differ on the question whether the theist has all the grounds for atheism that the atheist has. SGA holds that, relative to the theist's experience and limited knowledge, it is rational for him to believe what he does; but that, relative to the atheist's experience and less limited knowledge, it is only rational to believe that there is no God. PA holds that, even if there is no difference in the strength of their overall grounds, the theist and the atheist can each be rationally justified in believing what he does.

The distinction between the two forms of atheism can be sharpened by introducing the notion of a privileged evidential position. Let us say that one person A is in a privileged evidential position vis-à-vis another person B if A, in addition to having B's evidence for believing that P, has evidence not available to B which justifies A, as it would justify B if he had it, in believing that not-p. There are at least two ways in which A might come to be in this position. First, he might learn that there is an error in the grounds which B has for believing that p. For example, a passerby may think that a house is on fire because he sees what he takes to be smoke issuing from the basement windows, but the houseowner may know that what the passerby takes to be smoke is really steam from a broken pipe. In this kind of case, A has access to B's "grounds" for believing that p, but has good reason to believe that B's grounds are not what he takes them to be. In another kind of case, A may accept B's grounds at face value but, unlike B, be aware of other considerations which, taken into account, make it probable that the belief based on these grounds is false. The terrorist planting a bomb on an airplane seems to be in this position with respect to its passengers, for, while he presumably accepts their grounds for believing that they will disembark safely (the airline's exemplary safety record, let us say), he also knows something about this particular flight which they do not, something which justifies him, as it would justify them if they knew it, in believing that they are doomed. Of course, the notion of a privileged evidential position need not be restricted to different persons. A may himself come to believe that not-p as the result of discovering at a later time errors or significant omissions in his original grounds for believing that p.

The difference between the two forms of atheism can now be clarified as follows. As I am using the term, SGA is the position (a) that the atheist is in a privileged evidential position vis-à-vis the theist, and (b) that, as a result, the atheist is justified in believing that there is no God, as the theist is justified in believing the opposite. By contrast, PA is the position that, regardless of whether he has special grounds, the atheist is justified in believing that there is no God, as the theist is justified in believing that there is.

What shall we say about the strength of these two forms of atheism? I will argue for two major conclusions: (1) that SGA is coherent but uninteresting, unless the claim to special grounds can be upheld, which I believe it cannot; and (2) that PA is interesting but incoherent. Either way, the possibilities of friendly atheism seem to be very limited.

The obvious challenge to SGA is to make good the claim to speak from a superior evidential position to that of the theist. Historically, many atheists have risen to meet this challenge, but, to judge from the continuing controversial nature of their claims and the counterclaims of theists and agnostics, their success is highly questionable. Rowe himself makes a contribution to this venture when he argues from the amount and variety of human and animal suffering that it is extremely unlikely that all of this apparently pointless evil should turn out to be morally justified. But why should we accept this inference? It is not a necessary truth that a great number and variety of cases of suffering make it probable that the world contains morally gratuitous evil, and it is not a truth which Rowe or, as far as I know, any atheist has demonstrated.[7] Perhaps it is "reasonable" to accept the inference; at any rate, it is not demonstrably unreasonable, but that is cold comfort for the atheist, for it doesn't appear to be demonstrably unreasonable to reject the inference either. The limitation of Rowe's defense of atheism is that, while it may help to strengthen the conviction of other atheists, it is likely to leave the sophisticated theist untouched. It is interesting to enquire why this should be so, for it is certainly not a question of Rowe's competence. Indeed, I am tempted to say that, if Rowe can't make a watertight defense of atheism, no one can.

If we compare the atheist's case with a paradigm case of being in a special position to know, an interesting difference emerges. Suppose I believe that it is three o'clock because I have just looked at the electric clock on the wall and that is what the clock says. What I don't know, though you do, is that the power has been off for an hour and that, as a result, the clock is an hour off. Now you tell me about the power outage and perhaps confirm it by drawing my attention to a news report on the radio, and as a result I come to believe, as a matter of course, what you believe. But the case of the atheist and the theist is usually different. The atheist may regard himself as having, through cases of what he takes to be morally unjustified suffering, special grounds for his position, but when he proceeds to direct the theist's attention to these grounds, he finds that the theist remains as unconvinced as ever, for the theist is not unaware either that there is a great deal of suffering or that much of this suffering appears to be pointless, Consequently, whereas the atheist sees suffering as evidence for his position, the theist sees it as a phenomenon whose significance is easily misunderstood and can only be fully grasped within the overall context of theistic belief. Th$ theist's peculiar belief system allows him to assimilate the atheist's grounds without damage to itself.

It doesn't follow from the theist's ability to deflect the atheist's attack, of course, that the atheist is mistaken in taking suffering to be prima facie evidence against theism. For large-scale metaphysical theories may be so underdetermined by the facts that an ingenious thinker can, with sufficient patience and determination, weave a "likely account" to preserve any of them from clear cut refutation. But what does emerge from this sample of the confrontation between atheism and theism, I think, is that the atheist's position is dissimilar in an important respect to the familiar case where one party stands in a privileged evidential position to another party. The grave weakness in SGA is its failure to account for that difference.

Are the prospects for PA any brighter? Initially, they are, for PA, in not laying claim to know something which the theist does not, is not faced with the problem of justifying that claim. But PA is faced with another difficulty: it is not just paradoxical, as Rowe admits, but incoherent. My argument for this contention consists of two parts. First, I will give reasons for suggesting that Rowe's treatment of the paradox of friendly atheism resolves the paradox only by assimilating friendly atheism to SGA, and thereby fails to show that PA is a distinct conceptual possibility. Second, I will argue that, while there are certain conditions under which we can say to someone "You are mistaken, but justified in believing what you do," to say this in the absence of such conditions is to say something which is logically odd, if not absurd.

Rowe's proposed resolution of the paradox of friendly atheism emerges most clearly in the case of the damaged calculator, in which, presumably, you and I stand in evidential positions analogous to those of the theist and atheist. Rowe makes three claims regarding the calculator case:

(a) You have all my evidence for p. (i.e., the sum is x);
(b) I can reasonably believe that you are justified in believing that not p; and
(c) I have reason to believe that your grounds for not-p are not as telling as you are justified in taking them to be.

The trouble with this description is that the case presents us with a complex situation, part of which is described by (a) but not by (b) or (c), and another part of which is described by (b) and (c) but not by (a). The first part consists of my adding the numbers three times, arriving at the sum x each time, and reporting all of this to you. Up to this point it seems fair to say that you and I have "pretty much the same evidence" for the claim that the sum is x. To be sure, someone might object that I have the "evidence of my senses" whereas you have only my testimonial evidence, but that difference, while important in some contexts, is not important here. The important point to note is that so far you and I have no reason to disagree. Assuming that you have no reason to think that I am incompetent at simple arithmetic or in general untruthful or unreliable, I would not regard you as being justified if, in the face of my testimony and without countervailing grounds, you believed that the sum is not x. But perhaps it is essential for you to be right about the sum. This is where the second part of the case comes in. To double-check my calculation (not because you disbelieve it, but because you believe, as I do, that in general machine calculators are more reliable than human calculators), you whip out your calculator and tote up the numbers twice, arriving at the sum y both times. Not surprisingly, you now believe that the sum is not x. What you don't know at the time, though I do, is that your calculator is damaged. Because of the difference in our evidential positions at this point. I can now believe both that you are mistaken and justified in believing what you do. But it is no longer true to say of our overall evidential positions, as they bear upon the question of the correct sum, that you have all my evidence. Moreover, I would no longer regard you as justified if, after I disclosed to you my grounds for believing that your calculator has been damaged, you accepted the result obtained on your calculator without taking steps to determine its reliability.

Since Rowe's description of this case applies to different parts or phases of a complex situation, he fails to establish the general possibility of a position such as PA. What he establishes instead is the possibility of a position such as SGA, where one party is in a privileged evidential position vis-à-vis another party, but this possibility was never seriously in dispute. The paradoxical situation where person A believes both that person B has all of A's evidence for believing that p and that B is mistaken but justified in believing that not-p has still to be made out.

Of course, there are some situations under which it makes perfectly good sense to say to an opponent "You are mistaken, but justified in believing what you do." Three typical situations are the following. (1) We may think of our opponent as having reasonable grounds for his belief, but ones which in a particular situation are countervailed by other considerations of which he is (excusably) ignorant. The examples of the terrorist, the stopped clock, and the damaged calculator are cases of this kind. (2) We may think of our opponent as being mistaken about his grounds, where the mistake is reasonable for a person in his circumstances to make and where, but for the mistake, the alleged grounds would make it reasonable to believe what he does. So far the only example we have considered of this kind of case is that of the passerby who infers, on the basis of seeing what he takes to be smoke but what is really steam, that there is a fire. Another example would be that of the distracted person who misdials a telephone number and, when there is no response, concludes that the party he called is out. Sometimes a person's evidence is not what he takes it to be, as distinct from other times when his evidence is what he takes it to be but is, in some important respect, incomplete and misleading. Either way, we can think of him as being justified in believing what he does though what he believes is false. In thinking of him in this way, of course, we are assuming that, with respect to him, we occupy a privileged evidential position. (3) We may think that our opponent is *morally* justified in believing what he does, but not *epistemically* justified. For example, if Harry is in love with Tilly and believes in her innocence despite substantial evidence to the contrary, we may believe both that Tilly is guilty and that, out of loyalty, Harry is (morally) justified in refusing to accept this conclusion, at least as long as there is room for doubt.

In the absence of conditions such as those sketched above, it is difficult to make sense of the claim that someone has a mistaken but justified belief. For the claim pulls one in different directions. On one hand, to say to someone "You are mistaken in believing that not-p on grounds G" implies that one has access to grounds other than G-grounds which, if they do not rule out not-p, at least make it improbable. That is, it is to imply that one has access to grounds G' which create a strong presumption in favor of p. On the other hand, to say to someone "You are (rationally) justified in believing that not-p on grounds G" implies that one approves, or at least does not disapprove, of believing that not-p on these grounds, in the absence of countervailing considerations. That is, it is to imply that one's opponent has access to grounds which, considered by themselves, create at least a weak presumption in favor of not-p. Since the same grounds, taken as a totality, can hardly create a presumption both for and against p, it is apparent from this analysis that the grounds for calling a belief mistaken must be different from those for calling it justified.

We are left with the conclusion that, as far as PA is concerned, the atheist can be too friendly for his own good. He cannot admit that the theist is justified in rejecting atheism and yet has all the grounds that he, the atheist, has for accepting atheism, without undermining his own claim to be justified in accepting atheism. To make his position tolerable, the atheist must, as Rowe does, find some basis for differentiating between his grounds and those of the theist. But to do this is to abandon the paradoxical for the special grounds form of friendly atheism. The problem then is to defend the claim to be in a privileged evidential position against the attacks and counterclaims of theists and agnostics. As far as I know, neither Rowe nor any other atheist has solved that problem.

[1] See, for example, John Mackie, "Evil and Omnipotence," *Mind 64* (April, 1955).
[2] While St. Augustine and Leibniz are commonly associated with this position, it is by no means obsolete. A forceful contemporary exponent is Alvin Plantinga, *God, Freedom, and Evil* (Grand Rapids, Mich., 1974).
[3] *American Philosophical Quarterly*, 16 (Oct., 1979), 335-341. A simplified version may be found in Rowe's *Philosophy of Religion: An Introduction* (Encino, Calif., 1978), Ch. 6. The ancestral form of Rowe's approach may be found in Hume's *Dialogues Concerning Natural Religion*, Parts X and XI.
[4] Rowe, p. 336.
[5] Elsewhere Rowe undertakes to evaluate certain aspects of theism. See his *The Cosmological Argument* (Princeton, 1975) and *Philosophy of Religion: An Introduction* (Encino, Calif., 1978).
[6] Rowe, pp. 340-341, fn.
[7] For able critiques of Rowe's defense of atheism or the evidential form of the problem of evil, see Bruce Reichenbach, "The Inductive Argument from Evil," *American Philosophical Quarterly* 17 (July, 1980), 221-227; Delmas Lewis, "The Problem with the Problem of Evil," *Sophia (Australia)* 22 (April, 1983), 26-36; and Stephen J. Wykstra, "Difficulties in Rowe's Case for Atheism," forthcoming.

Reprinted with permission, "Was Hume an Atheist?" Hume Studies, Vol XIX, Number 1, April 1993.

WAS HUME AN ATHEIST?

Hume's philosophy of religion, as expressed in the *Dialogues Concerning Natural Religion,* the *Natural History of Religion,* and sections 10 and 11 of the *Enquiry Concerning Human Understanding*[1] invites a number of diverse interpretations. At one extreme are those who see Hume as an "atheist"[2] or "anti-theist."[3] At the other extreme are those who see Hume as some kind of theist, though not a classical or orthodox one.[4] In between are others for whom Hume is an "agnostic"[5] or "ironic skeptic."[6] Still a fourth interpretation can be found, according to which Hume "seems to vacillate hopelessly" in his view of religion;[7] in other words, no coherent philosophy of religion can be found in his work and so it is futile to look for one.

Of the four alternatives, it seems to me that the fourth, being less interesting philosophically and less to Hume's credit as a major philosopher, should be rejected unless by default no coherent case can be made for one of the other three. Since I believe that Hume's views about the nature and existence of God are complex, somewhat unconventional, but still coherent, I will concentrate on the title question. Before tackling that question directly, however, we need to clarify the meaning of the term "atheist" and its cognates. While an atheist is popularly defined as one who does not believe in God, this definition is inadequate for two reasons. First, while the absence of belief is sometimes treated as a synonym for disbelief, it is clear that the two are not the same. An infant does not believe in God, but that does not make him an atheist,[8] for, as yet, he does not have the linguistic competence to reflect on the question, Does God exist? Neither is the agnostic an atheist, for, though he has reflected on the question, he has not found reason to answer it affirmatively, like the theist, or negatively, like the atheist. For this reason, the atheist must be characterized more strongly, as one who *disbelieves* that God exists.

But even this stronger characterization is insufficient, for, as is well-known but perhaps less widely taken into account, there are many different conceptions of God, ranging from monotheism to polytheism, from belief in a perfect being to belief in a being who shares some human limitations, from deism to pantheism, and so on. Accordingly, it has become commonplace in philosophy to recognize at least two senses of the term "God": a narrow sense, signifying "a supremely good being, creator of but separate from and independent of the world, omnipotent, omniscient, eternal and self-existent";[9] and a wide sense, signifying one or more divine beings, personal or otherwise, manifesting extraordinary but perhaps not superlative properties. For short, we could call the narrow sense the standard concept of God, and belief in the existence of such a being *standard theism*.[10] And we could call the broad sense, applicable to any concept of the divine, the extended concept of God, and belief in the existence of such a beingfs) *extended theism*. On this account, standard theists will also be extended theists, but of course someone could be an extended theist without being a standard theist. Let us call such a person (for example, Epicurus, who denied, not that the Gods exist, but that they intervene in human affairs) a *limited theist*. It is important to note that the limited theist rejects standard theism but is not an atheist *simpliciter*.

How does recognition of these different forms of theism affect our understanding of atheism? There seem to be two major possibilities. One is to characterize atheism in the narrow sense as disbelief in standard theism; the other is to characterize it in the broad sense as disbelief in any form of theism, including limited theism. While either option is open, it seems to me that the latter is preferable. For if we say that anyone who rejects standard theism is an atheist, we will end up with the paradoxical result that many distinguished theists will turn out to be atheists. For example, while Charles Hartshorne is not a standard theist, insofar as he rejects the claim that God is absolutely perfect, omnipotent, and omniscient as this claim is ordinarily understood, it would surely be an abuse of the term to call him an "atheist." This is not to deny that historical examples of another kind can be found. Spinoza, perhaps the best-known western exponent of pantheism, was often attacked in his own time as an "atheist," but this charge strikes most modern readers of Spinoza as absurd. However it was in the past, it now appears that, at least in philosophical circles, the term "atheist" is generally restricted to people who disbelieve any form of theism, and this is the sense in which I propose to enquire whether Hume was an atheist.

To answer this question I propose to concentrate on Hume's major work on religion, the *Dialogues Concerning Natural Religion*. I believe that his other important works on the subject will be found to complement the position that emerges from the *Dialogues* rather than to oppose it. Despite the interpretive difficulties it presents, the special place of the *Dialogues* in Hume's philosophy of religion can hardly be denied. Although Hume had not completed revising the work at the time of his death in 1776, that is not because it was a last-minute effort. Norman Kemp Smith suggests that the original version was completed some time in the period 1751-57 and that Hume postponed publishing it in deference to friends who had seen it and recommended against publication.[11] The *Dialogues,* therefore, both are the fruit of Hume's mature years and express his long-held views on the subject. Moreover, Hume's anxiety to ensure publication of the work after his death argues that he regarded it as a worthy reflection of his views on the subject.[12] Since this work is a dialogue, however, there is the familiar difficulty of determining which (if any) of the three main characters— Philo, Cleanthes, or Demea—speaks for Hume. I shall take up this issue after a brief survey of the work's central argument.

The common impression that Hume was an atheist is not totally unfounded. The *Dialogues* itself puts forward three major objections to standard theism. First and most prominent is Philo's extensive and penetrating critique of the argument from design. This argument, along with its natural cousin, the cosmological argument, was a popular and scientific favourite in the eighteenth century, and a foundation for the whole enterprise of natural theology.[13] Hume qua Philo not only exposed the weaknesses of that argument, as popularly conceived at the time, but in doing so undermined confidence in the power of "reasoning from experience" to undertake so ambitious a task as deciphering the origin of worlds. Second, the cosmological argument also receives a bashing in the *Dialogues,* though the opponent this time is Cleanthes, using typical Hume-like arguments against the notion of necessary existence.

> I shall begin with observing, that there is an evident absurdity in pretending to demonstrate a matter of fact, or to prove it by any arguments *a priori.* Nothing is demonstrable, unless the contrary implies a contradiction. Nothing, that is distinctly conceivable, implies a contradiction. Whatever we conceive as existent, we can also conceive as non-existent. There is no being, therefore, whose non-existence implies a contradiction. Consequently there is no being, whose existence is demonstrable. (D 189)[14]

The work's third major objection to standard theism is once again delivered by Philo. Philo's critique of the argument from design develops into a version of the problem of evil. For the argument from design is supposed to show, not just that the world is the product of a superior intelligence, but that the Creator is, if not unlimited in power, wisdom, and goodness, at least "finitely perfect, though far exceeding mankind" (D 203). Against this claim Philo presses the point that, judging the properties of an unobserved object solely by reference to its observed effects, we can impute to the source of the world no more than the manifold imperfections experienced in this world. He challenges Cleanthes:

> Did I show you a house or palace, where there was not one apartment convenient or agreeable; where the windows, doors, fires, passages, stairs,

and the whole economy of the building were the source of noise, confusion, fatigue, darkness, and the extremes of heat and cold; you would certainly blame the contrivance, without any farther examination. The architect would in vain display his subtilty, and prove to you, that if this door or that window were altered, greater ills would ensue. What he says, may be strictly true: The alteration of one particular, while the other parts of the building remain, may only augment the inconveniencies. But still you would assert in general, that, if the architect had had skill and good intentions, he might have formed such a plan of the whole, and might have adjusted the parts in such a manner, as would have remedied all or most of these inconveniencies. His ignorance, or even your own ignorance of such a plan, will never convince you of the impossibility of it. If you find many inconveniencies and deformities in the building, you will always, without entering into any detail, condemn the architect. (D 204-5)

Philo's version of the problem of evil threatens not only natural religion but revealed religion as well, at least those forms of the latter which claim that God the Creator is omnicompetent: that is, omnipotent, omniscient, and wholly good. No wonder the orthodox Demea quits the field of battle "on some pretence or other" before the final round!

The apparently anti-theistic strains in the *Dialogues* can be found in Hume's other works on religion as well, including the *Natural History of Religion* and of course the famous essay "Of Miracles." The *Natural History* is one of the first major works to attempt to account for the phenomena of religious belief and practice in purely naturalistic terms, establishing a tradition which culminates in the psychologism of Nietzsche and Freud. Hume's polemical treatment of miracles not only suggests that belief in miracles is contrary to reason, but, since belief in miracles is one of the mainstays of belief in a divine revelation, also undercuts the claims of revealed religion. It is tempting to conclude from "Hume's three-pronged attack on religious orthodoxy" that Hume was a vigorous opponent of theism.[15]

At the same time, there are passages in both the *Dialogues* and the *Natural History* which support a different interpretation of Hume's aims. Despite their other differences, none of the principals in the *Dialogues* questions whether there is a God. At the outset of part 2, Demea sets the stage by identifying the real issue. Speaking of "the Being of a God ... that fundamental principle of all religion," Demea proclaims, "But this, I hope, is not, by any means, a question among us. No man; no man, at least, of common sense, I am persuaded, ever entertained a serious doubt with regard to a truth, so certain and self-evident. The question is not concerning the BEING, but the NATURE of GOD" (D 141). Comments follow about "the infirmities of human understanding," the divine nature as "mysterious to men," and "the temerity of prying into his nature and essence, decrees and attributes." Philo, commonly regarded as Hume's alter ego, responds by echoing Demea's remarks:

> But surely, where reasonable men treat these subjects, the question can never be concerning the *Being,* but only the *Nature* of the Deity. The former truth, as you well observe, is unquestionable and self-evident. ... But as all perfection is entirely relative, we ought never to imagine, that we comprehend the attributes of this divine Being, or to suppose, that his perfections have any analogy or likeness to the perfections of a human creature. ... He is infinitely superior to our limited view and comprehension; and is more the object of worship in the temple than of disputation in the schools. (D 142)

Cleanthes disagrees with Philo and Demea, but his disagreement concerns, not the existence of God, but the inscrutability of God's nature and the way in which his existence and nature can be known. There follows the famous analogy between the world and a machine:

Look round the world: contemplate the whole and every part of it: You will find it to be nothing but one great machine, subdivided into an infinite number of lesser machines, which again admit of subdivisions, to a degree beyond what human senses and faculties can trace and explain. All these various machines, and even their most minute parts, are adjusted to each other with an accuracy, which ravishes into admiration all men, who have ever contemplated them. The curious adapting of means to ends, throughout all nature, resembles exactly, though it much exceeds, the productions of human contrivance; of human design, thought, wisdom, and intelligence. Since therefore the effects resemble each other, we are led to infer, by all the rules of analogy, that the causes also resemble; and that the Author of Nature is somewhat similar to the mind of man; though possessed of much larger faculties, proportioned to the grandeur of the work, which he has executed. By this argument *a posteriori,* and by this argument alone, do we prove at once the existence of a Deity, and his similarity to human mind and intelligence. (D 143)

The stage is set for a discussion of Cleanthes' version of the argument from design, and Philo and Demea join forces in attacking the argument, though for different reasons. Demea is dismayed because, as he correctly perceives, the argument at best establishes no more than the *probability* that God exists, and thus takes a step in the direction of atheism. (If the conclusion is only probable, how probable is it: extremely probable, like the probability that every man will eventually die, or only barely more probable than not, like the probability of throwing a seven or higher on the next throw of the dice?) Philo attacks the argument for more interesting reasons, such as the important dissimilarities between the world and a machine (pt. 2); the unfortunate consequences for belief in a perfect being if the original analogy is taken seriously (pt. 5); the possibility of accounting for order in the world by no less strong analogies between the world and an animal body (pt. 6) or even a vegetable (pt. 7); and the dispensability of all such analogies in favour of the Epicurean hypothesis of "eternal revolutions of unguided matter" (pt. 8). The multiplication of cosmological hypotheses, each of which is plausible in itself but implausible in the face of its rivals, leads Philo to proclaim the triumph of scepticism:

> All religious systems, it is confessed, are subject to great and insuperable difficulties. Each disputant triumphs in his turn; while he carries on an offensive war, and exposes the absurdities, barbarities, and pernicious tenets of his antagonist. But all of them, on the whole, prepare a complete triumph for the *Sceptic,* who tells them, that no system ought ever to be embraced with regard to such subjects: For this plain reason, that no absurdity ought ever to be assented to with regard to any subject. A total suspense of judgement is here our only reasonable resource. And if every attack, as is commonly observed, and no defence, among Theologians, is successful; how complete must be *his* victory, who remains always, with all mankind, on the offensive, and has himself no fixed station or abiding city, which he is ever, on any occasion, obliged to defend? (D 186-87)

At this point the reader may begin to suspect that Philo was bluffing when he agreed with Demea that the question to be pursued was the nature, not the existence, of God. Is Philo's position not described by Pamphilus, the ostensible narrator of the *Dialogues,* as that of "careless scepticism" (D 128)? Before Philo is dismissed as a sceptic, however, two considerations should be kept in mind. The first is that Philo's scepticism may extend to views about the nature of God without extending to the belief that God exists. Of course, the two questions cannot be entirely separated. Whether one believes that God exists depends on what one takes God to be, but, as the tradition of the *uia negativa* suggests, one can believe the former without claiming to know very much about the positive nature of God, and this may be Philo's position, for it is entirely consonant with what he says elsewhere to his companions. The second point to keep in mind is that Philo's sceptical outburst occurs well before the end of the work. Philo has yet to present his version of the problem of evil, and the others to respond to it. If Philo is truly sceptical about the existence of God, we can expect that fact to emerge from the ensuing discussion of the problem of evil.

The discussion begins in part 10. Once again, Philo and Demea form a curious alliance: in opposition to Cleanthes, they emphasize the misery of animal and human existence and the corruptibility of human nature. The world is not, in their view, a good place, but the moral they draw from this point of agreement is very different. For Philo, the abundance and diversity of suffering in the world is proof against God's moral attributes:

> His power we allow infinite: whatever he wills is executed: but neither man nor any other animal are happy: therefore he does not will their happiness. His wisdom is infinite: he is never mistaken in chusing the means to any end: but the course of Nature tends not to human or animal felicity: therefore it is not established for that purpose. Through the whole compass of human knowledge, there are no inferences more certain and infallible than these. In what respect, then, do his benevolence and mercy resemble the benevolence and mercy of men? (D 198).

Demea resolves the problem of reconciling divine benevolence and human suffering by appealing to the so-called "porch" view: what appears to us here and now to be evil will, in the future and from a more comprehensive view, be seen to be a necessary part of a universal moral harmony and greater good:

> This world is but a point in comparison of the universe: this life but a moment in comparison of eternity. The present evil phenomena, therefore, are rectified in other regions, and in some future period of existence. And the eyes of men, being then opened to larger views of things, see the whole connection of general laws, and trace, with adoration, the benevolence and rectitude of the Deity, through all the mazes and intricacies of his

providence. (D 199).

Cleanthes responds to both arguments in a characteristic way. While siding with Demea against Philo on the question of divine benevolence, Cleanthes has no use for Demea's other-worldly theodicy and bursts out with the objection that his "arbitrary suppositions" have no experiential support, for a cause can be known only through its known effects, and the known effects in this case are the world's moral imperfections. Having rejected Demea's theodicy but retaining the traditional view of God's moral attributes, the empirical-minded Cleanthes sees no alternative but to deny his opponents' dark view of the world:

> The only method of supporting divine benevolence (and it is what I willingly embrace) is to deny absolutely the misery and wickedness of man. Your representations are exaggerated: Your melancholy views mostly fictitious: Your inferences contrary to fact and experience. Health is more common than sickness: Pleasure than pain: Happiness than misery. And for one vexation, which we. meet with, we attain, upon computation, a hundred enjoyments. (D 200)

Philo replies to Cleanthes with Hume's customary acuity. He scores three major points against the other's "method": (1) it undermines the foundation of religion by staking the claim to divine benevolence on the relative balance of human and animal pleasure over pain in this world—"a point which, from its very nature, must forever be uncertain"; (2) even if it could be shown that the world's stock of pleasure exceeds its stock of misery, "this is not, by any means, what we expect from infinite power, infinite wisdom, and infinite goodness," and so we return to the question why there is *any* misery in the world; and (3) even granting the *compatibility of* human misery and divine perfection, this would not be sufficient for the empirical theist's case. • Philo demands of Cleanthes:

You must *prove* these pure, unmixt, and uncontrollable attributes from the present mixt and confused phenomena, and from these alone. A hopeful undertaking! Were the phenomena ever so pure and unmixt, yet being finite, they would be insufficient for that purpose. How much more, where they are also so jarring and discordant? (D 201)

At this point, Philo seems to be satisfied that he has refuted the claim of natural religion to trace in God's handiwork the hallmarks of perfection. The measure of Philo's success is that, at the beginning of part 11, Cleanthes shifts his ground. Until now he has not disavowed standard theism, leaving it open to the reader to regard him as being, like Demea, a standard theist, but at this critical point in the discussion of the problem of evil, Cleanthes, like many another in the same position, falls back upon a form of limited theism. He admits the force of Philo's argument but invites him to consider an alternative conception of deity:

If we preserve human analogy, we must for ever find it impossible to reconcile any mixture of evil in the universe with infinite attributes; much less, can we ever prove the latter from the former. But supposing the Author of Nature to be finitely perfect, though far exceeding mankind; a satisfactory account may then be given of natural and moral evil, and every untoward phenomenon be explained and adjusted. A less evil may then be chosen, in order to avoid a greater: Inconveniencies be submitted to, in order to reach a desirable end: And in a word, benevolence, regulated by wisdom, and limited by necessity, may produce just such a world as the present. (D 203)

The God envisaged by Cleanthes at this point is not, of course, "that being than which none greater can be conceived," but may still be regarded as a kind of "supreme being," insofar as he is immeasurably more powerful, wise, and benevolent than any of his creatures.

Despite its more modest content, Philo finds little merit in the "supreme being" hypothesis. He attacks it by a series of moves, two of which are of special interest. First, he establishes a general framework in terms of which to evaluate the hypothesis, noting (1) that an intelligent being who accepted the hypothesis but was as yet unacquainted with the world would expect the world to be very different from what we actually find; (2) that, supposing this being to become acquainted with the world, he would be surprised at the discrepancy between what he expected and what he found, but not on that account prepared to jettison the hypothesis, provided it was originally based on "very solid argument" and he was aware of the limitations of his intelligence; and (3) that, supposing the being to become acquainted with the world but not antecedently convinced of the hypothesis and left to test its truth from the appearance of things (as in the typical human case), he would never, however aware of the limits of his understanding, find reason to conclude that the hypothesis was true. Otherwise put, Philo maintains that, given the world as we experience it, the supreme being hypothesis has a low probability. This probability is not so low that it could not be countervailed by independent evidence conferring a very high degree of probability upon the supreme being hypothesis, but, in the absence of such evidence, the presumption against the hypothesis stands.

Philo's second interesting move in attacking Cleanthes' hypothesis is to focus attention on natural rather than on moral evil. If the intention of Philo's creator was to use the fact of evil to expose a fundamental weakness in the argument from design, he could not have chosen a more effective strategy. Moral evil, as evil done by men, invites the presumption that it is evil which deserves punishment, either as retribution for the evil done or as a means to reform the evildoer or to deter others from succumbing to similar temptation. But deserved evil, it might be said, is no real evil, only apparent evil. At face value, therefore, moral evil does not pose a problem for the theist's belief in the goodness and justice of God. But it is otherwise with certain forms of natural evil. Perhaps some natural evils can be regarded as the natural consequence of human wrongdoing (as land erosion and famine may result from irresponsible use of natural resources); others as "punishment" for wrongdoing (as venereal disease was once thought to be the natural punishment for sexual promiscuity); and still others as tests of faith (Job suffers through no fault of his own) and as ways of building character (Bunyan's pilgrim progresses only through meeting and overcoming obstacles), but human ingenuity is strained to account for the remainder of natural evil, especially that which has nothing to do with human agency or which befalls all sentient beings, including very young children and animals, normally considered to be moral "innocents." Not surprisingly, Philo dwells on natural evil of this kind—evil which does not appear to human reason to be, in the least degree, necessary or unavoidable. If Philo is correct in suggesting that such evil is avoidable, at least for a being equipped with exemplary power, wisdom, and goodness, the profusion of such evil in nature creates a presumption (though not a proof) that, if some being is responsible for the totality we call the world, that being is less than exemplary in some important respect.

Philo, for one, has no doubt that this world, taken as a whole, is deeply and avoidably flawed. "Look round this universe," he directs his companions.

> What an immense profusion of beings, animated and organized, sensible and active! You admire this prodigious variety and fecundity. But inspect a little more narrowly these living existences, the only beings worth regarding. How hostile and destructive to each other! How insufficient all of them for their own happiness! How contemptible or odious to the spectator! The whole presents nothing but the idea of a blind Nature, impregnated by a great vivifying principle, and pouring forth from her lap, without discernment or parental care, her maimed and abortive children. (D 211)

Philo's dark view leads him to frame four hypotheses regarding "the first causes of the universe": that they are endowed with perfect goodness, perfect malice, a mixture of goodness and malice, or none of these qualities. He dismisses the first two possibilities on the ground that the world's "mixed phenomena"— its apparent mixture of good and evil—cannot be accounted for by principles which, respectively, allow for either no evil or no goodness. And he dismisses the third possibility on the ground that it is opposed by "the uniformity and steadiness of general laws." Of the fourth possibility, he says only that it "seems by far the most probable," presumably because it alone allows both for the lawlikeness of nature and for the mixture of good and evil to be found in the world. While allowing that this conclusion may be rejected, he insists that, as long as any evil exists in the universe, it must be accounted for by natural religion. To the great dismay of his companions, who now suspect him of being a secret enemy of religion, Philo concludes with the admonition:

> So long as there is any vice at all in the universe, it will very much puzzle you Anthropomorphites, how to account for it. You must assign a cause for it, without having recourse to the first cause. But as every effect must have a cause, and that cause another; you must either carry on the progression *in infinitum,* or rest on that original principle, who is the ultimate cause of all things. (D 212).

At this point, discussion of the problem of evil is broken off and Demea shortly departs, leaving Philo and Cleanthes to wrap up the discussion in part 12. And what a strange wrap-up it is! Up to now Philo's penetrating critique of the argument from design, his devastating treatment of the problem of evil and the "supreme being" hypothesis, and certainly his friends' suspicions as to the sincerity of his original proclamation regarding religion, have all combined to create the impression that Philo has emerged in his true colours as an opponent of theism. But this initial impression is not sustained in the final part of the *Dialogues.* On the contrary, we find that Philo appears to reverse himself and, *in agreement with Cleanthes,* to insist that some positive theistic conclusions can be drawn from the analogy between the order of nature and the works of man. A string of claims concerning "design" flow this time from Philo, who calls them his "unfeigned sentiments on this subject." Philo begins with a confession:

> You in particular, CLEANTHES, with whom I live in unreserved intimacy; you are sensible, that, notwithstanding the freedom of my conversation, and my love of singular arguments, no one has a deeper sense of religion impressed on his mind, or pays more profound adoration to the divine Being, as he discovers himself to reason, in the inexplicable contrivance and artifice of Nature. A purpose, an intention, a design strikes every where the most careless, the most stupid thinker; and no man can be so hardened in absurd systems, as at all times to reject it. (D 214)

Philo goes on to suggest that the dispute between theists and atheists may be regarded as a *verbal* one. This surprising notion, new to the discussion so far, is supported by two observations: one, that some controversies are forever beyond resolution; and two, that these are "controversies concerning the degrees of any quality or circumstance." A debate about whether Hannibal was a general or Cleopatra a Queen of Egypt can be settled, for there is a difference in *kind* between being and not being a general or between being and not being Queen of Egypt, but when it comes to the question whether Hannibal was a great general or Cleopatra very beautiful, the dispute is of another kind, for greatness and beauty are matters of degree, and the degree of either which satisfies one disputant may not satisfy another. Philo hypothesizes that the dispute between theists and atheists (as also that between dogmatists and sceptics) is of this nature, and that as a result the dispute is unresolvable and therefore "verbal" (D 216-18).

Superficially, it may look as if the theist and atheist are debating whether there is, or is not, a God, but as Philo sees it, the crux of the matter is the degree of difference between the human and the divine mind—a difference which tends to be maximized by the theist and minimized to the point of being whittled away by the atheist. Philo's advice to both parties is, in effect, "to agree to disagree"— that is, to treat the matter as if it were a difference of taste or inclination. In other words, if you are overwhelmed by the difference between the world and what you presume to be its cause, call this source God; but if you consider the cause of the world, if it has a cause, to be very much like this world, call it nature rather than God. But in any case, recognize and respect the inclination of another to view the difference of which you are both aware in a different manner. "Consider then," Philo says, "where the real point of controversy lies, and if you cannot lay aside your disputes, endeavour, at least, to cure yourselves of your animosity" (D 218-19).

Philo's ambivalent attitude toward the argument from design resurfaces in his final speech, where he both suggests that the arguments for the proposition, *"That the cause or causes of order in the universe probably bear some remote analogy to human intelligence"* (D 227, Hume's emphasis), exceed the objections against it, and at the same time draws attention to its limitations. For, in Philo's view, unlike Cleanthes', the proposition is too "undefined" to imply that the cause or causes of order in the universe have any specific attribute other than intelligence, or that human beings ought to conduct themselves in any particular way. Unless we dismiss Philo's remarks in part 12 as pure posturing (making him a liar when he speaks of revealing his "unfeigned sentiments"), we are left with the conclusion that Philo is no atheist, at least in the wide sense of the term, but a limited theist. His is a more attenuated form of limited theism than we find in Cleanthes and certainly very different from the orthodox theism of Demea, but it is not for that reason the total rejection of theism. Philo, at least, is no atheist.

Philo's arguments elsewhere in the *Dialogues* also point to that conclusion. The aim of his devastating critique of the argument from design is to show, not that there is no God, but that, if there is a God, we cannot infer from the empirical evidence alone that he is perfectly or even supremely powerful, wise, and good. Again, the proper conclusion of Philo's version of the problem of evil is, not that there is no God, but that God, if he exists, is limited in some important respect—

if notin power and intelligence, then in goodness. At no point does Philo maintain, as some later day atheists have done, that God and evil are incompatible. For this reason his position cannot be attacked, as theirs can, by proofs of their compatibility.[16]

Indeed, if we compare Philo's and Cleanthes' conceptions of God, we will find that the chief point on which they differ has to do with the question of God's moral attributes and their implications for human conduct. Cleanthes is prepared to allow that God is "finitely perfect" but still as benevolent as it is possible for such a being to be. As we saw in his critique of the supreme being hypothesis, however, Philo challenges the claim, not that God is supremely powerful or wise, but that he is benevolent to the same degree, at least as human beings understand benevolence. Indeed, Philo contemplates the possibility that the origin of the world (assuming it to have an origin) is morally neutral, being neither benevolent nor malevolent. It seems fair to say, therefore, that Philo and Cleanthes are both limited theists, though Philo advances a more minimal version of that position. On this interpretation, the principal issue in the *Dialogues* turns out to be, as was affirmed at the beginning of part 2, the nature rather than the existence of God. The battle of wits is not between two theists and an atheist, so much as it is between three theists holding strikingly different conceptions of God and different conceptions of how that nature is to be known.

But what does this interpretation of the *Dialogues* tell us about Hume's own philosophy of religion? We cannot afford to assume that any one of the three principals is speaking for Hume. But there is evidence elsewhere in Hume's work that his position is probably closest to that of Philo. Three striking "parallels" may be noted. First and most obviously, Hume like Philo was a sceptic. Hume's scepticism was perhaps more general in that it extended to all manner of beliefs, including beliefs not questioned by Philo, such as belief in the external world, the uniformity of nature, and the continuity of the self; but scepticism with regard to the epistemic grounds of these beliefs did not lead Hume to disavow them, any more than scepticism with regard to the epistemic grounds of Demea's and Cleanthes' theistic beliefs led Philo to disavow theism completely. And further, just as Hume's scepticism as regards "common sense" beliefs led him to reconstrue these beliefs, to determine what could be salvaged from them, so Philo's scepticism led him, in a similar manner, to reconstrue more traditional forms of theism. The outcome of this strategy was for Hume a naturalistic theory of belief, and for Philo a minimalist version of theism. In any case, Philo's sceptical outlook is one of the hallmarks of his character.[17] Pamphilus' prologue contrasts the "careless scepticism' of Philo with the "accurate philosophical turn" of Cleanthes and the "rigid inflexible orthodoxy" of Demea. "Careless" is to be construed here, of course, not as sloppy but as carefree, since the sceptic traditionally achieves intellectual quietude *(ataraxia)* by recognizing that, as a general rule, as much can be said for, as against, any given philosophical proposition.

A second parallel can be found in the fact that several of Philo's objections to the argument from design can be found in another of Hume's works, the *Enquiry Concerning Human Understanding,* where Hume once again casts the matter in the form of an imaginary dialogue—this time between himself, who at one point pretends to be Epicurus addressing a group of Athenian citizens, and "a friend who loves sceptical paradoxes." Taken to task by the Athenians for denying "a providence and a future state," Hume-as-Epicurus once again points out the most serious limitation of the design argument: in inferring from the order in the world that, like the order to be found in human contrivances, it is probably the result of a designing intelligence, there is no reason to attribute to the hypothetical designer greater qualities of workmanship than we find in the work itself:

> When we infer any particular cause from an effect, we must proportion the one to the other, and can never be allowed to ascribe to the cause any qualities, but what are exactly sufficient to produce the effect. A body of ten ounces raised in any scale may serve as a proof, that the counterbalancing

weight exceeds ten ounces; but can never afford a reason that it exceeds a hundred.[18]

While exposing the limitations of this favourite argument for natural theology, however, Hume-as-Epicurus, like Philo, stops short of maintaining that the "religious hypothesis" is false.

A third parallel between Philo and Hume can be found in Hume's second major work on the subject, the *Natural History of Religion*. While we may hesitate to identify any particular *persona* in the *Dialogues* with the author, Hume is speaking in *propria persona* in the former work, and his views bear a strong resemblance to Philo's endorsement of a minimalist version of the argument from design. To give but two samples;

> The whole frame of nature bespeaks an intelligent author; and no rational enquirer can, after serious reflection, suspend his belief a moment with regard to the primary principles of genuine Theism and Religion.[19]

> *A little philosophy,* says lord BACON, *makes men atheists: A great deal reconciles them to religion.* For men, being taught, by superstitious prejudices, to lay the stress on a wrong place; when that fails them, and they discover, by a little reflection, that the course of nature is regular and uniform, their whole faith totters, and falls to ruin. But being taught, by more reflection, that this very regularity and uniformity is the strongest proof of design and of a supreme intelligence, they return to that belief, which they had deserted; and they are now able to establish it on a firmer and more durable foundation. (NHR 4:329, Hume's emphasis)

While it is true that the *Natural History* ends on an agnostic note ("The whole is a riddle, an aenigma, an inexplicable mystery" [NHR 4:363]), it should be noted that agnosticism, understood as the view that we lack sufficient *evidence* to pass judgement on the issue dividing theists and atheists, is compatible both with certain forms of theism, such as fideism and the rejection of evidentialism, and with the general Humean position that the source of certain basic beliefs, such as the belief that like causes have like effects (and vice versa?), is natural feeling or sentiment rather than reason. Hume was a limited theist in more than one respect: not only did he subscribe to a watered-down version of theism, but he subscribed to that in a tentative way, in sharp contrast to the full commitment generally associated with standard theism. Because of this doubly limited theism, it may seem that Hume's support for the "religious hypothesis" is too tenuous to warrant the label. Tenuous as it may be, however, it still shows that Hume was no atheist, as the term is being used in this paper.

In addition to the shared philosophical views of Hume and Philo, there is some biographical evidence that Hume associated himself most closely with Philo. Writing to his good friend Gilbert Elliot in 1751, to whom he sent a sample of the work, Hume said: "Had it been my good Fortune to live near you, I shou'd have taken on me the Character of Philo, in the Dialogue, which you'll own I could have supported naturally enough: And you would not have been averse to that of Cleanthes."[20] In the same letter, however, Hume claims "I make Cleanthes the Hero of the Dialogue," and requests his friend's assistance in strengthening Cleanthes' side of the argument. The juxtaposition of these two remarks is puzzling: if Philo is, so to speak, Hume's spokesman, why does Hume say that another character is the hero? Another puzzle for the Hume-Philo connection is Hume's remark, in a letter to the publisher William Strahan shortly before Hume's death, "I there [in the *Dialogues]* introduce a Sceptic, who is indeed refuted, and at last gives up the Argument, nay only confesses that he was only amusing himself by all these cavils" *{Letters,* 2:323). Can Philo be said to be speaking for his author if the latter confesses that Philo has been refuted?

The resolution of this perplexity may perhaps be found in distinguishing between the actual and the nominal hero of the *Dialogues*. The nominal hero of the work is Cleanthes, for Pamphilus, passing judgment upon the now completed discussion, awards the palm of victory to Cleanthes, second place to Philo, and third place to Demea. "I confess," he says, "that, upon a serious review of the whole, I cannot but think, that PHILO'S principles are more probable than DEMEA S; but that those of CLEANTHES approach still nearer to the truth" (D 228). Pamphilus' judgement is not remarkable; he is, after all, a pupil of Cleanthes and a younger philosopher, who, apart from his role as scribe, plays no part in the discussion he records. When Hume reported that Cleanthes was the hero and that the sceptic was refuted, he was, of course, reporting the situation from Pamphilus' point of view. But there is no need for us, or for Hume for that matter, to share this point of view. The delicious irony of the ending of the *Dialogues* is that a second-rate thinker is made to appear the victor, in the judgement of that thinker's pupil!

Whether or not these literary loose-ends can be tied up, they do not affect the main point of this paper: that Hume, however sceptical, playful, and ironic, did not totally disbelieve in some form of theism. Indeed, if Cleanthes is regarded as the actual victor in the *Dialogues,* the case for regarding Hume as a theist will be even more solid. Since part 12 reveals that Philo and Cleanthes share much common ground, in accepting some form of theism, though Philo's is clearly more attenuated than that of Cleanthes, it does not matter, for present purposes, which one is to be regarded as the real hero. There is in this work, however, a real loser. Demea, in abandoning the field to his opponents, suggests that the case for standard theism cannot be sustained. The *Dialogues,* therefore, leave no place for standard theism.

What about section 10 of the first *Enquiry,* the famous chapter "Of Miracles," originally written for the *Treatise of Human Nature* but suppressed out of fear of giving offense to the leading churchmen of Hume's early literary career? Though this piece is often regarded as an attack on a major bulwark of religious belief, it is not necessarily an attack on theism as such. The famous line, "We may conclude that the Christian Religion not only was at first attended with miracles, but even at this day cannot be believed by any reasonable person without one," is usually understood as an instance of Hume's celebrated irony. But Hume does not stop there. He goes on to add something upon which many theists would insist: "Mere reason is insufficient to convince us of its [Christianity's] veracity: And whoever is moved by *Faith* to assent to it, is conscious of a continued miracle in his own person, which subverts all the principles of his understanding, and gives him a determination to believe what is most contrary to custom and experience" (E 131). In other words, reason is opposed to belief in miracles and other Christian beliefs, but Hume does not go on to the further conclusion that therefore these beliefs are, or probably are, false. Is that because he regarded the conclusion as too obvious to be worth stating, or because he was unwilling or unable to go so far? While the essay itself remains ambivalent, Hume's other works on the philosophy of religion yield clues as to his intentions. Hume regarded standard theism with deep suspicion, but his belief in some form of theism was never entirely abandoned.

Despite the evidence we have considered, the conclusion that Hume was a theist will not go unchallenged. If the matter were so simple, it would hardly be a matter of debate among Hume scholars. Several objections to the theistic interpretation of Hume are certain to be made. Without claiming that these are the only or the most important ones, I shall conclude by briefly considering and replying to four objections which come naturally to mind.

First, to begin with a biographical note, there is evidence that Hume disavowed any belief in religion. James Boswell, the great biographer of Dr. Samuel Johnson, reported the following conversation with Hume towards the end of Hume's life:

He said he never had entertained any beleif [sic] in Religion since he began to read Locke and Clarke. I asked him if he was not religious when he was young. He said he was. ... He then said flatly that the Morality of every Religion was bad, and, I really thought, was not jocular when he said 'that when he heard a man was religious, he concluded he was a rascal, though he had known some instances of very good men being religious.'[21]

Taking this account at face value, isn't it clear that Hume was no theist from youth onward? The answer is no, for the religious beliefs which Hume disavowed were very different from the minimal theism expressed in the *Dialogues* and the *Natural History*. Hume was brought up as a strict Calvinist, an interpretation of Christianity which emphasized the subservience of man to God and laid down demanding rules for every phase of conduct. In Locke and Clarke, Hume would have encountered a more liberal form of Christianity, but one which he could not bring himself to accept, for Locke had used an empirical argument and Clarke an a priori argument to demonstrate the existence of the God of standard theism, when Hume had come to conclude that no such argument could succeed. "And 'tis not long ago," Hume wrote Gilbert Elliot in 1751, "that I bum'd an old Manuscript Book, wrote before I was twenty; which contain'd, Page after Page, the gradual progress of my Thoughts on that head. It began with an anxious Search after Arguments, to confirm the common Opinion: Doubts stole in, dissipated, return'd, were again dissipated, return'd again; and it was a perpetual Struggle of a restless Imagination against Inclination, perhaps against Reason" *(Letters,* 1:153). Hume did lose his religious beliefs, then, but these beliefs were so different from his later beliefs on the subject of a limited deity, that there is no need to suppose that he was talking about the same thing. Hume no doubt was aware that most theists of his day would regard his thought as irreligious.

Second, it may be asked: given Hume's penetrating critique of natural religion and his apparent animus toward revealed religion, why did Hume hang on to a *remnant* of theism? Why not go all the way and become, if not an atheist, at least an agnostic? Before suggesting an answer, I think we should note the tendentious nature of these questions. From the standpoint of standard theism, Hume could, of course, be described as hanging on to a remnant of that belief; but, having a regard to the rich and varied tapestry of extended theism, there is no call to describe Hume's position in that way. Hume's theory was not a "residue" of theism; it was another form of cheism. As such some thinkers may find it intellectually unattractive and prefer a barer world-landscape, but that is not to say that Hume was unable to free himself from the grip of religious orthodoxy.

A partial explanation of Hume's limited theism may lie in the sceptical tradition of which Hume was a part.[22] Hume was sceptical not only of the dogmatic assurance of theologians like Dr. Samuel Clarke and Bishop Joseph Butler in his own time, but also of the equally dogmatic denials of the French *philosophes*. Reason, on his view, could not reach so far as the origin of worlds, having no experience of such a singular event. As he saw it, both orthodox religion and atheistic materialism outran the bounds of reason and experience. Such a view would seem to recommend suspension ofbelief—agnosticism—buthere another element in traditional scepticism came into play. The ancient sceptics realized that, at least in the sphere of action, a man could not remain fixed in a state of indecision, and so they recommended that the sceptic guide his conduct by the customs of society and shape his beliefs by the appearances of things, but always without the dogmatism of the "true believer." Since Hume lived within a nominally Christian society and was evidently personally struck by the appearance of design in nature, at a time before this apparent design could be scientifically explained in nonteleological and nontheological terms, it is not surprising that he inclined toward a theistic worldview, even though he saw that there were no compelling rational grounds for this outlook. Neither did the ancient sceptics disavow everything they found no evidential reason to accept.

A third objection to the theistic interpretation of Hume may be put as follows: what is God-like about the being whose portrait emerges from the tatters of the design argument? For this is the portrait of a being who is limited in some important respect—if not in power and wisdom, then in goodness—and whose existence, while more probable than not, is far from certain. Needless to say, such a being is far removed from the God of standard theism, and to a lesser extent from the supreme being of Cleanthes and deists in general. In that case, one may object, would it warrant the attitude of worship, adoration, and devotion associated with more robust forms of theism? Indeed, if such a being existed, why call it "God" ? Wouldn't it be just another extraordinary object—as amazing in its own way as perhaps Mozart was as a musical prodigy, but otherwise scarcely sacred or holy?

Dissatisfaction with Hume's form of theism has been expressed by a number of commentators. T. H. Huxley writes:

> But, if we turn from the *Natural History of Religion,* to the *Treatise,* the *Enquiry,* and the *Dialogues,* the story of what happened to the ass laden with salt, who took to the water, irresistibly suggests itself. Hume's theism, such as it is, dissolves away in the dialectic river, until nothing is left but the verbal sack in which it was contained.[23]

Ernest C. Mossner, author of Hume's definitive biography and champion of the man and of the philosopher, is nevertheless not impressed by Hume's watered-down concept of God. As he sums it up:

> The *a posteriori* argument from design proves only that the being of a God is faintly analogous to human intelligence and this analogy, faint as it is, cannot be transferred to the moral attributes of God. So the conduct of human life remains unaffected. The ' religious hypothesis ' is impotent. There is no natural religion.[24]

Norman Kemp Smith, in a similar vein, writes:

Hume's attitude to true religion can therefore be summed up in the threefold thesis: (1) that it consists exclusively in *intellectual* assent to the "somewhat ambiguous, at least undefined" proposition, 'God exists'; (2) that the 'God' here affirmed is not God as ordinarily understood; and (3) as a corollary from (1) and (2), that religion ought not to have, and when 'true' and 'genuine' does not have, any influence on human conduct—beyond, that is to say, its intellectual effects, as rendering the mind immune to superstition and fanaticism.[25]

These and other comments express an understandable disappointment with Hume's version of theism, but the reason for the disappointment should be considered. We (Westerners?) are disappointed, perhaps, because historically we have come to think of theism as if it were synonymous with standard theism, and so any concept of the divine which falls short of the standard of perfection in all respects may well strike us as unworthy of its object. Transfixed by the notion of "that being than whom none greater can be conceived," the reader may feel that only such a being could be God, and that anything less does not deserve the name. By this standard, of course, even Cleanthes' "finitely perfect God" will fail to qualify, and even more so the God delineated by Hume's Philo. The fault may lie, however, not with the deists (of whom Hume may be counted a member), but with the exclusionary standard employed. Examine the multiplicity of concepts of God to be found in various cultures or devised by ingenious philosophers, and you will find that theism—theism in general—has never been committed exclusively to the concept of a perfect God, nor has worship of and devotion to divinity been restricted in such manner. To take but one famous example, the Lord's voice as the voice out of the whirlwind responds to Job's lamentations over his bitter fate by stressing, not God's justice and benevolence, but his power, majesty, and wisdom. And Job responds, not by saying, "Well, in that case, you aren't God" or, "You may be God, but you aren't just," but by acknowledging his own limitations:

> I know that thou canst do every thing, and that no thought can be withholden from thee. Who is he that hideth counsel without knowledge? therefore have I uttered that I understood not; things too wonderful for me, which I knew not. ... Wherefore I abhor myself, and repent in dust and ashes.[25]

The spirit of self-abasement is lacking in Philo, but he too stresses the "adorably mysterious and incomprehensible nature of the Supreme Being." (D 143)

Seen against the broad perspective of theism in general, Hume's concept of God will be seen not as an aberration in an otherwise uniform tradition, but as another variation on a rich theme running throughout the "religions of man." No doubt Hume's concept of God can be so watered down that little is left but the name, but does it have to be? God could be limited and still be, in comparison with humans, enormously more powerful and wise, and perhaps morally better, than the best of men. The notion that only an omnicompetent being can be worthy of worship, devotion, and reverence may only be a prejudice of perfection. If it is possible to revere someone like Socrates, Jesus, or Gandhi, who presumably were less than perfect but possessed certain powers and moral qualities far in excess of the ordinary, it is possible to revere a being who, compared to the greatest of human beings, may be like the sun to a candle. Hume's God, like Job's God, is not the God of standard theism, but for all that it is still a being in whom one can trace the lineaments of the divine.

A fourth and final objection to be considered here calls into question whether Hume's version of theism, as proposed in this paper, is consistent with his empiricist theory of knowledge and naturalistic metaphysics. As every reader of Hume's first *Enquiry* knows, that work concludes with the famous passage:

> When we run over libraries, persuaded of these principles [broadly, that matters of fact can be known only through experience and never through

demonstrative reasoni ng], what havoc must we make? If we take in our hand any volume; of divinity or school metaphysics, for instance; let us ask, *Does it contain any abstract reasoning concerning quantity or number?* No. *Does it contain any experimental reasoning concerning matter of fact and existence?* No. Commit it then to the flames: for it can contain nothing but sophistry and illusion. (E 165, Hume's emphasis)

This passage anticipates the logical positivists' verification principle: a statement is literally meaningful if and only if it is either analytic (intuitively or demonstratively certain, for Hume) or empirically verifiable (testable by experimental reasoning, for Hume).[26] Given such a principle, how could Hume consistently believe in God, unless "God" was for him just another name for the presumptive original source of natural order? It seems that, to be consistent, Hume could be a theist in name only; or, if he was more than a nominal theist, that his philosophy of religion would be inconsistent with his empirical and naturalistic philosophy. Therefore, it may be argued, either Hume was not consistent in his overall philosophy or he was not, as I have maintained, a theist.

This objection raises a number of difficult issues, but I will concentrate here on the question of consistency. While it would be extravagant to insist that Hume's philosophy was throughly consistent,[27] there is no need to accuse Hume of *gross* inconsistency between his philosophy of religion and his epistemology and metaphysics. Nor is there a need to concede that he was a theist in name only. The dilemma "inconsistent or nontheist" is spurious, for it presumes, what is false, that a theist cannot be an empiricist or naturalist. No doubt many forms of theism are inconsistent with an empiricist epistemology or a naturalistic metaphysics, for they postulate a transcendent God who is different in kind from and independent of his creation and whose presence can be known directly only through self-revelation; but this is not true of all forms of theism. Perhaps the best-known example to the contrary is John Stuart Mill, who characterizes God in terms which are remarkably similar to Hume's Philo:

A being of great but limited power, how or by what limited we cannot even conjecture; of great, and perhaps unlimited, intelligence, but perhaps also more narrowly limited than his power; who desires and pays some regard to the happiness of his creatures, but who seems to have other motives of action which he cares more for, and who can hardly be supposed to have created the universe for that purpose alone. Such is the Deity whom natural religion points to; and any idea of God more captivating than this comes only from human wishes or from the teaching of either real or imaginary revelation.[28]

One may object, of course, that Mill himself was inconsistent in uniting theism with empiricism and naturalism, and so his example proves nothing with regard to Hume. Perhaps this objection can be sustained by construing "empiricism" and "naturalism" so narrowly as to exclude whatever goes beyond "immediate sense experience" or whatever is other than a "sense datum," but such a narrow construal of these terms invites the difficulties to which the verification principle in its more stringent formulation was early exposed. When "empiricism" is used more broadly to cover whatever can be known directly through observation or indirectly from observation through legitimated rules of inference, and "naturalism" to cover the content of whatever is accessible in either of these ways, there is no occasion to deny their compatibility with theism. A thought-experiment will, I think, confirm this. According to the Gospels, Jesus Christ was observed to do a number of remarkable things: to restore a dead man to life, to walk on water, to reappear to his disciples after his death, and so on. Suppose that all these things were true and, moreover, that we had personally observed them to be true: given only this and the information that Jesus was conceived by a virgin and claimed to have a special mission and to stand in a special relation to God, it would not be unreasonable for us to believe that Jesus was, if not God, at least a God or one who possessed divine powers. Yet in this story, our principal evidence for believing what we do is the "evidence of our senses" and the person about whom we have this belief is someone who, in other respects, resembles ourselves and other human beings.

If this story fails to be convincing, imagine that you know someone who can, at your request, restore the dead to life, the aged to the prime of life, and the sick to health; who can arrest hurricanes, floods, and other natural disasters; who can bring life-giving rains to drought- stricken areas, temperate warmth to frigid wastes, and cooling breezes to sun-scorched lands; who can, for the benefit of human and other sentient beings, stay the tides, the motion of the moon and other heavenly bodies. Who would deny that such a being, if he existed and we had no reason to think that we were dreaming or hallucinating, had God-like powers or was divine?[29] And in believing this, on the basis of our own observation, would we not be embracing a form of theism?

I conclude that Hume's theism is not inconsistent with his empiricist methodology and naturalistic worldview. If a different opinion has sometimes prevailed, that may be accounted for by the tendency, noted above, to assimilate theism to standard theism. Since opponents of standard theism are often regarded as atheists, it is not surprising that Hume should have been so regarded by many of his contemporaries and successors, despite the fact that he never identified himself with that group. And the reason he did not do so was not intellectual or social timidity, but the fact that, as he probably realized, he was not a member of that group. The story is told that, at a dinner party hosted by the Baron d'Holbach in Paris, Hume remarked that, "He did not believe in atheists, that he had never seen any," to which the Baron replied that, of the eighteen other persons present, fifteen were atheists and the other three hadn't made up their minds.[30] While this anecdote may tell something about the difference between English and French intellectual circles in the eighteenth century, it also, I think, tells us something about David Hume. He was not disingenuous when he spoke as he did.

Grateful acknowledgement is made for the original impetus for this project, provided by the NEH Summer Research Seminar "Church, State, and Moral

Control in Early Modern Europe," directed by William E. Monter, Northwestern University, 1990; and also to two colleagues, Roger Wertheimer and Charles Hughes, who read and commented upon earlier drafts of this paper.

California State University, Long Beach

---

[1] "Of Miracles," and "Of a particular Providence and of a future State." Other relevant works include the essays "Of Superstition and Enthusiasm," "On Suicide," and "On the Immortality of the Soul."
[2] See, for example, Antony Flew, *The Presumption of Atheism* (London, 1976), 52.
[3] Timothy A. Mitchell, *David Hume's Anti-Theistic Views* (Lanham, MD, 1986).
[4] Nelson Pike, ed., *Dialogues Concerning Natural Religion* (Indianapolis, 1970), 222-38. Also J. C. A. Gaskin, *Hume's Philosophy of Religion*, 2d ed. (Atlantic Highlands, N. J., 1988), 130.
[5] James Noxon, "Hume's Agnosticism," in *Hume*, ed. V. C. Chappell (Garden City, N.Y., 1966), 361-83.
[6] John Valdimir Price, *The Ironic Hume* (Austin, 1965), 152.
[7] Keith E. Yandell, "Hume on Religious Belief," in *Hume: A Re-Evaluation*, ed. Donald W. Livingston and James T. King (New York, 1976), 109.
[8] Except, possibly, for those who believe in original sin!
[9] William L. Rowe, *Philosophy of Religion: An Introduction* (Dickenson, 1978), 14.
[10] The term is borrowed from William L. Rowe, "Evil and the Theistic Hypothesis: A Response to Wykstra," *International Journal for Philosophy of Religion* 16 (1984): 95. Rowe contrasts "standard theism" with "expanded theism" and "restricted theism," but the latter do not correspond to my distinction between "extended theism" and "limited theism."
[11] David Hume, *Dialogues Concerning Natural Religion*, ed. Norman Kemp Smith (Indianapolis, 1947), 57 (hereafter cited as "D"). Hume's friends were probably concerned lest the work's anti-religious tone alienate its readers and so set back the author's growing literary reputation.
[12] For an account of the difficulties Hume encountered in arranging for its publication, see Ernest C. Mossner, *The Life of David Hume*, 2d ed. (Oxford, 1980), 592-93.
[13] For an historical overview of the role of the argument from design in eighteenth century science, see Robert H. Hurlbutt, *Hume, Newton, and the Design Argument*, rev. ed. (Lincoln, NB, 1985).
[14] For Hume's own statement, see *the Enquiry Concerning Human Understanding*, sec. 12, pt. 3.
[15] The phrase is quoted from Richard Wollheim, ed.*Hume on Religion* (Cleveland, 1969), 25. Wollheim insists, however, that "Hume never called himself an atheist, nor thought of himself as one."
[16] See, for example, Alvin Plantinga's reply to J. L. Mackie in *God, Freedom and Evil* (Grand Rapids, 1977), 12-55.

[17] John Valdimir Price maintains that the choice of the name "Philo" for the sceptic in the *Dialogues* was not accidental, since Philo (160-80 B.C.) was the founder of the so-called fourth Academy and academic philosophy had become synonymous with sceptical philosophy:

[18] David Hume, *Enquiries Concerning Human Understanding and Concerning the Principles of Morals*, ed. L. A. Selby-Bigge, 3d ed., rev., ed. P. H. Nidditch (Oxford, 1975), 136 (hereafter cited as "E").

[19] David Hume, Natural History of Religion, in *The Philosophical Works*, ed. T. H. Green and T. H. Grose, 4 vols. (Darmstadt, 1964), 4:309 (hereafter cited as "NHR").

[20] David Hume, *The Letters of David Hume*, ed. J. Y. T. Grieg, 2 vols. (Oxford, 1932), 1:154 (hereafter cited as Letters).

[21] *Boswell* Papers, 12:227. Quoted in Mossner, *The Life of David Hume* (above, n. 12), 517.

[22] See Richard H. Popkin, "David Hume: His Pyrrhonism and His Critique of Pyrrhonism," in *The High Road to Pyrrhonism*, ed. Richard A. Watson and James E. Force (San Diego, 1980), 103-31.

[23] Quoted in Norman Kemp Smith, "Hume's Views Regarding Religion in General," in *Dialogues*, 22.

[24] Ernest C. Mossner, "Hume and the Legacy of the Dialogues," in *David Hume: Bicentenary Papers* ed. G. P. Morice (Edinburgh, 1977), 18.

[25] Job 42:2-6.

[26] See A. J. Ayer, "Introduction," in *Language, Truth and Logic*, 2d ed. (New York, 1946).

[27] What philosopher's thought does not undergo development and modification over time? I assume that Hume's thought is coherent if his central tenets, as expressed in his mature work, are not incoherent.

[28] John Stuart Mill, *Three Essays on Religion* (AMS Press, 1970), 195.

[29] So far this story leaves open the possibility that the being in question is only your amanuensis, and that you are the god ultimately responsible for these extraordinary events. To block this possibility we may need to incorporate the proviso that this being does not always obey your requests—notably, when they are destructive or perpetrated by you only as a means of self- aggrandizement.

[30] Mossner, *The Life of David Hume* (above, n. 12), 483.

ARE WE DESCARTES' BABIES?

Paul Bloom, psychology professor at Yale University, uses the story of Descartes' baby to explore the way we humans tend to think about ourselves.[1] According to this story, which of course may be apocryphal, the French philosopher and mathematician Descartes is reputed to have carried around in his travels a chest containing a lifesize doll resembling his illegitimate daughter who died young. The sea captain who discovered the doll was horrified by what he saw and threw the doll overboard. Presumably, he could not abide the thought of something which looked human but, like other animals, lacked a soul. Even today many people find the idea of a soulless human—what could be called a soul zombie—repulsive. But in Bloom's view that is what modern science says of us: we are fleshy creatures who often find ourselves appalled by the idea that we might be nothing but flesh. As Bloom puts it succinctly, "We are Descartes' babies."[2] While he finds this view of our innermost nature "profoundly troubling," he apparently shares it.

By contrast, the dualistic conception of man still prevails in many parts of the globe. Dualism, as I understand it, involves three central ideas, none of which is endorsed by modern science: (1) we humans have nonphysical souls as well as physical bodies; (2) our souls are capable of existing apart from our bodies, and hence can survive when our bodies perish; and (3) having a soul is what distinguishes us from other animals. Familiar as these ideas are in the great monotheistic religions, Bloom attributes them, not to religious indoctrination, but to the way we naturally view ourselves and the world from the time we were babies. That is why he calls it "intuitive dualism" or "common sense dualism."[3]

Like more traditional forms of dualism, common sense dualism, or CSD as we might call it for short, holds that human beings are embodied souls and not just embodied creatures. That term of course can be understood in more than one way. When we speak of someone being "the soul of the party," or of the loss of so many souls in a shipwreck, or of an empty hall with no soul in sight, we need not be dualists in the intended sense, for the context makes it clear that we are referring to humans. For the dualist the soul is more than that: as one dictionary says, it is "the spiritual or immaterial part of a person, regarded as immortal." When dualists affirm and naturalists deny that souls exist, that is the issue at stake.

Bloom supports the naturalistic view of science with evidence drawn from his study of the cognitive development of young children. For example, research involving babies' looking-times shows that babies look longer at people than at other kinds of object, suggesting that they find them more interesting. They apparently regard members of their own species as *special:* they are not just another kind of animal. Babies prefer to look at faces and apparently expect them to move in ways that are appropriate responses to their own actions. They even look longer at patterns of light that move in a human-looking fashion or circles of light appearing to chase each other. "Babies," Bloom says, "are natural dualists."[4] The minds of young children are not limited to what they can see. Bloom notes that they give greater weight to hidden internal properties than to observable external features of objects. It is easy for them to think that someone is happy or sad simply by looking at his or her face. They attribute thoughts and feelings to their pets. Children are also "promiscuous teleologists": they attribute purpose and intention to many things, regardless of whether they are artifacts or natural kinds. "What's it for?" and "What's it supposed to do?" are natural questions, whether asked of a tuning fork or a turtle. Children think there must be a reason for their existence, not having learned to distinguish reason as cause from reason as motive. Children name their creations after their intentions, rather than after their likeness to the objects represented. A scribble can represent smoke, however unlike the real stuff. Children live as much in their minds as they do in their bodies.

Bloom's claim that we are "natural dualists" is plausible in the light of such evidence. Nevertheless, it is clear that, on his view, modern scientific findings give no support to the dualistic picture of man. It looks as if we are disposed to espouse a view of ourselves that has no basis in reality. Such an eventuality would not be unprecedented. Modern science has often shown that our naive view of the world is deceptive. As Bertrand Russell famously put it, "Naive realism leads to science, and science shows that naive realism is false." Is the same thing true of our naive view of ourselves?

From an evolutionary point of view, the answer appears to be yes. Bloom himself reminds us that, to the extent evolution aims at anything, it is survival and reproduction, not truth.[5] We can expect that, where the truth of beliefs is important to survival, as in learning what foods are safe to eat, natural selection will favor true beliefs. By the same token, it will favor false beliefs that are conducive to one's survival, like belief in the power of totems. The naturalness of a belief seems to be an index to its attractiveness, not to its superior cognitive value. Babies show more interest in members of their own species for the same reason that young children see purpose and intention in everything: by and large these traits promote their survival. Being wrong in thinking that a tree has intentions is less dangerous than being unable to read a rival's intentions.

Though Bloom opposes the soul hypothesis, he is aware that a number of reasons can be adduced on its behalf, apart from religion. He draws our attention to four of these reasons and leaves it to the reader—in this case myself—to assess their merit. Accordingly, I propose to review his account, as I understand it, and to show that, while it may appear to create a presumption in favor of dualism, in the end it fails to deliver the goods. Finally, I hope to show that, when certain misunderstandings are cleared away, the naturalistic view of *Homo sapiens* remains in the field.

First, the dualist can point to a curious linguistic fact: in speaking of our bodies, we use the language of possession. We say "I have a body," not "I am a body," as if, like other things we own, we were different from our bodies. As Bloom says, we feel as if we occupy our bodies, much as we might occupy a house. Personal identity seems to be independent of the particular state of a body. John Doe can lose a limb or a sense or an organ without losing his personal identity, so in principle why can't he lose his *body* without losing his identity as a person? In that case of course we couldn't access his presence in the same way, but change of access needn't involve change of existence. We could dub this the ownership argument. I have developed it more fully than Bloom does, but I think it is in the spirit (no pun intended) of what he says.

Second, the dualist can appeal to familiar facts about bodily change and psychological continuity. To give it a name, we could call it the argument from persistence through change. As everyone knows, our bodies undergo profound physical changes during the course of a lifetime, from infancy to maturity and old age. But our sense of self or personal identity remains relatively constant throughout that lifetime. We feel that we are the same person now as we were as a child, despite the constant replacement of the cells which make up our bodies. Mutable body, persistent self—how could the two be the same?

It might be objected that incremental changes do occur in the self as fresh experiences are added and old memories are lost. While that is true, it does not ordinarily affect our sense of personal identity. We feel that we are the same person now as before, despite variations in the content of our experience and memory, just as in watching a movie we feel ourselves to be the same viewer throughout the changing scenes. The self persists in the midst of change, so how can it be identical to the body?

Third, the dualist can carry body/self independence one step further. Whatever the reality of *post mortem* survival, we can easily conceive of surviving the death of our body but it is harder, if not impossible, to conceive of the self as no longer existing.[6] For example, it seems easy to imagine witnessing our own funeral, but in doing so we are still thinking of ourselves as being secretly present. Believers in reincarnation go so far as to imagine prenatal existence or existence in some non-bodily form between lives. On the familiar principle that what is clearly conceivable is possible, life after death is a real possibility, not a mere figment of the imagination. Call this the argument from conceivability.

The conceivability argument has a particular fascination for philosophers, perhaps because it can yield far-reaching conclusions from the comfort of one's armchair. Descartes is a famous example. Finding he could not doubt his existence as a thinking, conscious being, whereas he could doubt his existence as a body, Descartes concluded that his mind was separate from and more easily known than his body, and further, that mind and matter were distinct substances, the essence of mind being consciousness and the essence of matter extension. Bloom's version of the argument is more modest but, like its famous predecessor, it implies that, amongst natural beings, man is unique in being more than a body and thereby able to survive death.

Fourth and finally, the dualist can appeal to the argument from disparity.[7] It seems undeniable that certain things are true of our bodies which aren't true of *us,* and vice versa. For example, your body consists of millions of cells and several pints of blood, but it would be distinctly odd to say that *you* consist of millions of cells and several pints of blood. Again, you may be thinking of your twenty-first birthday bash, or wanting to see reforms in the health care system, or expecting a call from your stockbroker, but it sounds crazy to say that your body is doing any of these things. For *you* are the agent, not your body or any of its parts. Likewise for your personal states. You are (say) a grandparent and a retired teacher but that doesn't mean your body or any part of it is a grandparent or retired teacher. Over and over, things seem to be true of *you* which aren't true of your body, so how can you be identical with your body? For the two to be identical, whatever is true of one would have to be true of the other, and vice versa, but that is precisely what we don't find. Ergo, you are not your body.

It is time to assess these arguments. By and large, they proceed from plausible points: that we speak of having bodies, that we think of the inner self as persisting through change, that we can imagine ourselves as existing apart from our bodies, and that things are true of us which aren't true of our bodies. Admittedly, these claims are loosely stated, but allowing for that I have no wish to deny any of them. The problem with them lies elsewhere. One and all, for reasons to be explained below, they leap to a conclusion which is not warranted by the evidence for it. If this is correct, we have no reason to accept the validity of dualism as an account of the way things really are.

(1) It is true, as Bloom claims, that we speak of our bodies as if they were possessions. But it is a mistake to think you have a body in the same sense in which you have a house. For if you own a house, you can transfer ownership of it to another party, by sale, exchange, or gift. But you can't transfer ownership of your body in any of these ways without transferring yourself, as in selling yourself into slavery. In the former case, you remain distinct from the property you transfer; in the latter case, you do not. You go with your body in a way you do not go with your house.

There are two apparent exceptions. One, people sometimes speak of a woman as "selling her body," where they mean, not that she has sold *herself* into slavery, but that she has "sold" the use of her body for a limited purpose and a limited time. She has not sold her body so much as rented out the use of it.

Such talk should be recognized for what it is, a figure of speech, like the expression "the foot of a mountain."

A more challenging case is the way we speak of a corpse. When John Doe dies, we tend to say that we are burying, not him, but his *remains*. We speak of him as having "passed away" or "departed," as if he still exists but has merely left our presence. It is easy to dismiss such expressions as euphemisms, like asking for the restroom when you want the toilet, but a better explanation is available. If John Doe were buried alive, as he might be in a snow avalanche, it would be appropriate to say that the avalanche buried *him,* not his remains. John Doe goes where his living body goes, so when he dies in the ordinary way, it is his remains we bury, not him.

In any case, it is clear that having a body does not rule out being a body, any more than having a personality rules out being a personality. Why then do we speak of having rather than of being a body? Perhaps because of a tendency to think that, if we are bodies, we must be "mere" bodies, whereas we like to think that we are "more" than bodies. But the first doesn't follow and the second can be accommodated without subscribing to dualism. While a human corpse is a mere body, a living human is not, for the latter is an agent whereas the former no longer is. In turn, that difference explains how we are more than bodies. We are more, not because our bodies are animated by souls, but because we are agents who can use our bodies to act and bring about desired changes in our environment.

(2) The question of persistence through change is complicated by the fact that identity comes in more than one flavor. Qualitative identity is different from numerical or quantitative identity. Two things x and y are qualitatively identical if and only if every property possessed by x is also possessed by y, and vice versa. "As alike as two peas in a pod" is a rough expression of this sense of identity—

rough because it is based on limited powers of observation. There may be micro-differences we cannot observe and certainly there are differences in spatial location, but ignoring those, the two peas appear to be qualitatively identical. Mix them up, and we could not reliably tell one from the other.

Numerical identity is another matter. Our look-alike peas are not one but two, and a body can change over time without ceasing to be the same body. Looking at a picture of himself as a baby, an old man can say "That was me seventy years ago," and he is right, for his elderly body is spatially and temporally continuous with his infant body, in the sense that, if we could follow it moment by moment, we would see it developing by degrees from one stage to the other. Qualitatively different as they are in many respects, the infant and the old man are numerically one and the same.

These different senses of identity allow us to make sense of the phenomenon of persistence through change. Though the body undergoes qualitative change over time, these changes take place in what is numerically the same body. Therefore, there is a perfectly good sense in which, contrary to dualism, the body does not change but "persists." And there is a perfectly good sense in which, again contrary to dualism, the so-called "self both persists and undergoes change. Numerically, we can speak of the same psychological self; but qualitatively, we can speak of the ever-changing "stream of consciousness": the same stream but different contents. Persistence and change can be found in both body and self.

(3) I turn now to the claim that we can imagine existing apart from our bodies, as in imagining that we are observing our own funeral or, better, our own cremains. This claim can be disputed on the ground that we can't observe something without using our eyes, and since by hypothesis our eyes no longer exist in the imagined state, it is incoherent, like the notion of traveling backward

in time to prevent one's parents from meeting. I won't press this difficulty, but it seems to me there are other hurdles, even if we accept the hypothesis in question.

How do I know in the imaginary scenario that the body in the casket or the cremains are mine? Why couldn't it be a simulacrum of me or the cremains of someone else? I can stipulate that they are mine, of course, but, as Abraham Lincoln pointed out, stipulating that a tail is a leg doesn't change the fact that a dog has four legs. Unlike fiction, biology and forensics can't be done by fiat.

Is it possible to exist without a body? That depends on what is meant by "possible." Like many philosophical terms, "possible" has more than one meaning. A state of affairs is *logically* possible if it can be described without inconsistency; *physically* possible if it is consistent with the laws of nature; and *epistemically* possible if it is not ruled out by what we know. Existing without a body, like building a frictionless machine, may be logically possible but it doesn't follow that it is physically or epistemically possible. On the basis of what we know about human brains and bodies, neither bodiless existence nor frictionless machines appear to be physically or epistemically possible. It is small consolation, then, to be told that they are still possible—only logically possible. You might as well say that it's possible for you to have lunch on the moon tomorrow.

(4) One problem remains: the discrepancy between what is true about a person and what is true about his body. Descartes would never have considered the personal report "I think, therefore I am" as equivalent to the physical report "My body thinks, therefore my body exists." How then can he—the person—be identical with his body— the stuff? At face value, it is impossible, for "I think" does not mean "My body thinks." Nevertheless, it might be the case that when I think, my body, or at least that part of it called my brain, is doing the thinking.

The key to this possibility is the notion of contingent identity. Science shows that something which is known under one description can in fact be identical—numerically identical—to something known under a different description. Astronomers have discovered that the "star" first seen in the evening is one and the same as the "star" last seen in the morning, the planet Venus. So the evening star turns out to be the morning star and both stars turn out to be the same planet. Who would have guessed this from the meaning of the original expressions?

Chemists have discovered that water is a molecule made up of two elements, two atoms of hydrogen and one of oxygen. So water is H_2O, the same thing under different descriptions. "Water" of course doesn't mean "H_2O"—people knew what water is long before the advent of modern chemistry—but that doesn't prevent water from being contingently identical to H_2O. In a similar vein, I suggest, it is possible for "I think" to be contingently identical to "My body thinks" or, to be more exact, "My brain thinks."

It is fair to ask, however, whether this possibility is more than another vacuous logical possibility. Is it possible, in the stronger physical or epistemic sense, that "I think" and "My brain thinks" are contingently identical? In my opinion, it is not only possible but probable. As is well-known, brain imaging studies show that blood flow increases significantly in specific areas of the brain when the patient engages in certain kinds of cognitive activity. The correlation between cognition and blood flow suggests that the two have a physical basis, as the monist proposes, rather than a nonphysical basis, as the dualist postulates. If cognition were the work of a nonphysical agent, as the dualist supposes, it is hard to see why it would be correlated with changes in the brain. For that matter, why would an immaterial soul be embodied in the first place? The mystery of ensoulment is surely as great as the mystery of consciousness.

It may be objected, however, that you are more than the physical body you see reflected in the mirror at a given moment. True, you are more than *that* but it doesn't follow that you aren't your body. What you see in that reflection is the present stage of a body that is itself the outcome of past stages of that body, together with its capacities and dispositions, and also the platform of its dimly descried future stages. Like the proverbial iceberg, the portion you see is only a fraction of what is there. That is why there is more to you than what you see reflected in the mirror. Like a melody, in effect you are a being extended in time and not just in space. Just as books can look much alike and yet vary enormously in content, so human bodies can look much alike and yet house remarkably diverse biographies. The biography of a body can be called a "soul" but that doesn't make it a soul in any but the weak sense.

Despite the many critiques of dualism, it is pervasive in everyday life and speech. For example, as a rule only humans are called persons, and food places cater to customers but post signs like "No animals allowed." A human who commits an atrocity is condemned as "only an animal," as if we were anything but animals, and we dignify our species by calling our best behavior "humane," as if it were typical of us. Virtually every society regards humans as superior to animals, and hundreds of millions of religious people believe that humans, unlike animals, have a special relationship with the divine. Our language reflects the incipient dualism of the great majority of our species, but that doesn't mean that it reflects the reality of our situation. Just as we continue to speak of "sunrise" and "sunset" without taking these terms literally, we may learn to speak of "humans and animals" without supposing that we are talking about two different kinds of entity.

While people pay lip-service to the idea that humans are animals, this idea isn't clear, for the term "animals" is multiply ambiguous. *The Concise Canadian Oxford Dictionary* points out that an animal can be any of these things:

- A living organism which feeds on organic matter, usually one with specialized sense-organs and a nervous system, and able to respond quickly to stimuli.

- Such an organism other than man.

- A brutish or uncivilized person.

- Informal: a person or thing of any kind ("no such animal as Superman").

Clearly, only the first of these senses applies to humans in general, and even that applies only to living humans. (Obviously, a human corpse isn't "a living organism").

Even when the proposition "Humans are animals" (call this H) is clarified, however, many people resist its implications. In discussing it with others, I have found that H is often confused with other claims and sometimes rejected for the wrong reason. In particular, H doesn't mean that humans are (1) the same as animals; (2) nothing but animals; or (3) no better than animals. None of these things is so.

Certainly, H does not say that humans are the same as animals. What it says is that the class of humans is included as a proper subset in the class of animals, no less than the class of dogs and every other species of animal. To say that one class is included in another as a proper subset is to rule out the possibility that the two classes are "the same."

Does H say that humans are nothing but animals? Not exactly. It does say that no humans are not animals, but it doesn't say that members of the species Homo sapiens are no different from other species of animals, for H allows for species-typical differences as well as genus-wide similarities. To use an analogy, consider the statement "Bats are mammals." Clearly, it implies that no bats are not mammals, but it doesn't imply that bats are no different from other mammals. On the contrary, bats are unique in being mammals that fly and echolocate. By the same token, humans can be like animals in certain ways—e.g. feeding on organic matter—and still be quite unlike them in other ways—e.g. typically capable of speech, reason, and morality. H is quite compatible with that complex fact.

As for qualitative comparisons, it makes no sense to say that humans are, or are not, superior to animals. The truth is that we can't compare the value of two things without comparing them in a certain respect. It makes no sense to say that an orange is, or is not, better than a pencil; if you're hungry, the orange is better; if you're not hungry but need to write down a telephone number, the pencil is better. Their overall value to literate humans may well be equal, but not so to fructivores.

If humans are superior to animals, therefore, it looks as if they must be superior in some respect, but what can that be? Religion provides one obvious candidate: humans are superior because they alone are made in the image of God. Granted certain beliefs about God, that claim may well be true but what if there is no God or there are multiple gods none of whom is worthy of moral approbation? The claim "If God exists, we are superior to animals" seems to share the logic of "If I win the grand lottery, I'll be a millionaire." The truth of the conditional does not ensure the truth of either its antecedent or its consequent, only that if its antecedent is true, so must be its consequent. The likelihood of either being true may be very low indeed.

Dualistic theories provide a fertile ground for *speciesism*—the belief in human superiority leading to the exploitation of animals.[8] If every human has some valuable attribute that no animal has, it is natural to think that humans are better than animals. The problem is to find something of great worth that belongs to all and only humans.. Many candidates have been proposed but none seems to stand up to scrutiny. To be sure, there are common human attributes—being conceived by human parents and carrying a human genetic code, for instance—but it is hard to see what makes them especially valuable without begging the question. And there are valuable traits that may be exhibited only by humans—compassion, a sense of justice, and intellectual curiosity, to mention a few—but obviously not by every human. In the face of this difficulty, dualists often resort to metaphysical entities: Plato's rational soul, the Cartesian ego, Kant's noumenal self. Can the naturalist be blamed for suspecting that such intellectual artifacts have a self-serving role?

When it is properly understood, nothing seems plainer than the fact that humans and animals exhibit both similarities and differences. As we move down the evolutionary ladder, the similarities become fewer but never entirely disappear. We share DNA and other basic biological features with even the lowly amoeba. Hence it is no misnomer to speak of the human animal or of humans and other animals.

To some, this conception of our species will appear base and degrading. That is because their conception of animals in general is base and degrading. If we are animals, whatever we are capable of is what some animals are capable of. If we are capable of altruism, creativity, learning, and spirituality, so are some animals. Equally, if we can be base, violent, cruel, and mindless, so can some animals. Being animals takes nothing away from us that was there before.

The dualist may take exception. He may say that as animals we have lost our immortal souls and hope of a better life to come. But he is wrong. If belief in reincarnation and karma is right, animals too are part of the same cosmic process as ourselves. In fact, we might have been animals ourselves in the past. If on the other hand this belief is mistaken, no animal can enjoy such blessings, and neither can we. In neither case have we lost something we really had.

Nothing displays our similarities with and differences from animals more clearly than the consumption of food. Humans and other animals need to eat and generally pursue food avidly, but the foods they eat and their ways of securing and eating them are remarkably diverse. Unlike other animals, humans are variety seeking omnivores who regularly cook their food, eat with special implements, and often treat eating as a social occasion. Concentrating on these differences, we might think that humans and animals are utterly different, but we have only to consider the role of food in preserving and satisfying both creatures--their neediness, dependency, and vulnerability--to realize how much they also share.

Feeding is only one half of the digestive process; the other half is elimination. Having taken in food and drink, animals have to excrete what their bodies cannot assimilate. I was once in a lab class where the instructor described the animal body as "a tube within a tube," one end for feeding and the other for waste disposal. The model fits the human body as well. We are nowhere so animal-like as in having to dispose of our waste. Perhaps that is why most of us prefer to perform that function in private.

The strength of naturalism, as opposed to dualism, is that it can do justice to both the more and the less lofty aspects of our nature. If children are natural dualists, as Bloom insists, that may be because they have awakened to our ambivalent state. But it is a fact of embodiment, not of ensoulment. If it is a mystery how the water of brain activity turns into the wine of consciousness, as Colin McGinn puts it, it is no less a mystery how it is done by the soul. In the end, the naturalist can say of the soul what Laplace is reputed to have said in response to Napoleon's complaint about the absence of God in the latest system of astronomy: "Sire, I did not need that hypothesis."

References

[1] Bloom, Paul. *Descartes' Baby: How the Science of Child Development Explains What Makes Us Human* (Basic Books c2004).
[2] Ibid., p. xiii.
[3] Ibid., p. 177.
[4] Ibid., p. xiii.
[5] Ibid., p. 222.
[6] Ibid., p. 191.
[7] Ibid., p. 195.
[8] Ibid., p. 207.
[9] The argument from persistence through change can be regarded as a particular form of the argument from disparity.
[10] *The Concise Canadian Oxford Dictionary.*

CAN NATURALISM ALLOW FOR EVIL?

According to Ivan Karamazov, "If there were no God, everything would be permitted." This bold claim has been challenged before,[1] but it warrants another look. If everything in a Godless universe is permitted, nothing would be impermissible and so nothing would be evil, but is that the case? Confronted by the problem of evil, theists have, more than naturalists, struggled with the idea of evil and its role in the divine plan. While naturalists do not face that problem, they face another: in a Godless universe, does it make sense to speak of evil?

Theists from Leibniz on have generally recognized two major kinds of evil: *moral evil,* for which human beings or at least free agents are responsible, and *natural evil,* which is variously regarded as the result of moral evil, as the punishment for sin, as the test of faith, as the opportunity for "soul-making," or as the result of the impersonal working of the laws of nature. Absent a divine legislator who judges and dispenses rewards and punishments in the afterlife, how can naturalists make sense of either kind of evil? My object in this paper is to sketch a theory which allows for moral and natural evil and yet is compatible with the naturalistic perspective. I will also argue that, while it cannot be proven, the naturalistic conception of evil enjoys certain advantages over its rival.

First, some notes about terminology. By a theory of evil, I mean a branch of the general theory of value. It is no part of my purpose to outline, let alone develop, such a general theory here. Nevertheless, no view of evil from either perspective can get away from some account of the nature of disvalue or negative value, the extremity of which presumably is the locus of evil. For my limited purpose I propose to take *suffering,* in the broad sense which includes both experiential and nonexperiential forms, as the primary form of disvalue, and the typical causes of suffering, such as the harm caused by human agents and by natural disasters, as its secondary form.

This is not to say, of course, that suffering always has negative value, for it may be deserved, as when offenses are justly punished, or it may promote a greater value, as when the travails of labor are crowned with success, or it may prevent a greater evil, as when surgery is performed to save a life. But when in fact the agent neither deserves to suffer nor derives compensating benefit from his suffering, I suggest that he is entitled to regard it as undesirable, uncalled for, and pointless. In short, if his life would be better without it, his suffering is without value, and may even have significant disvalue, for him. It may have value for others, if they wish to see him suffer, but then we may want to ask why they so wish and whether their wishes deserve to be respected.

Finally, what makes a theory of evil theistic or naturalistic? By the theistic theory of evil, I mean the kind of account found, by and large, in the three major Western religions-Judaism, Christianity, and Islam—and also vigorously defended by many theistic philosophers from St. Augustine to the present day. Some critics treat it as the religious view of evil but that is an overgeneralization, for theism is not the whole of religion. Whether the theistic theory of evil applies to other forms of religion is a separate question, not taken up here.

As for the naturalistic theory of evil, I take it to be the common form of a family of views which are united at least in rejecting the worldview of theism. Whereas theists generally look to scripture for inspiration and enlightenment, naturalists today generally look to modern science for support, if not inspiration, with special attention to biology and the behavioral sciences, supplemented by dollops of world and human history. To qualify as naturalistic, a theory of evil must be compatible with the worldview of scientific naturalism, the historical successor to earlier forms of materialism.

Theism and naturalism offer very different pictures of the world and our place in it. Theism in effect postulates two worlds, the first of which is entirely dependent on the second: the Natural World, the created world of things and creatures, and the Supernatural World, consisting of the supreme creator, God, and perhaps the devil and lesser functionaries. Human beings, alone perhaps of all natural creatures, are supposed to partake of both worlds, having a foot, so to speak, in the natural world, and a soul in the supernatural.

But what do I mean by "supernatural"? Perhaps it is best understood by contrast with the natural: a supernatural agent, if one exists, is neither constituted by physical "stuff" nor bound by the laws of nature. Nevertheless, he/she/it has the peculiarity of being able to interact with ordinary things and creatures and thereby to control their fate, not unlike the author of tales about fictional characters. Just as Dickens can send his hero to the guillotine or not, a supernatural agent can control the fate of a real person in a way that natural agents cannot.

A supernatural agent has another important dimension, which can be brought out by contrast with the human situation. Human beings make their wishes known and exchange information by means of speaking, writing, reporting, documenting, and so on, which have nothing to do with the supernatural. Our daily commerce with the world and each other can be described as thoroughly naturalistic. Barring the intervention of the supernatural, we have no access to information about that realm to distinguish it from wishful thinking, speculation, or other activities of the imagination. Once the supernatural breaks in, however, the picture changes. By means of revelation, prophecy, and the working of miracles, the supernatural discloses, or is claimed to disclose, hitherto unsuspected information beyond the natural order—information which supposedly is vital to our salvation and future wellbeing. As such, the supernatural is conceived to be a special source of knowledge, different from and superior to our ordinary sources of knowledge.

The metaphysical and epistemological implications of naturalism, by contrast, are very different. Naturalism can be regarded as a one-world or many-worlds view. It is a one-world view insofar as it has no place for the supernatural, but a many-worlds view insofar as it countenances the reality of many kinds of thing, including the animate and the inanimate, the mindful and the mindless, the conscious and the self-conscious, the concrete and the abstract, the particular and the universal, and so on. Naturalism is not materialism, understood as the thesis that nothing but matter and the void exist. But it is like materialism in holding that one thing—in this case, nature in all its diversity and plurality—is all there is. Naturalists can and do disagree about many things—e.g. how best to understand minds, abstract entities, and universals—but, to the extent they are naturalists, they see no need to introduce the supernatural as part of their explanation of the natural. Their answer to theists, like that of Laplace to his sovereign, is simply "Sire, I do not need that hypothesis."

Not surprisingly, naturalism has no need for the theist's revelations, prophecies, and miracle stories; his division of the human being into body and soul; and his deliverances about the afterlife, the day of judgment, and heaven and hell. Nevertheless, the naturalist is left with a budget of residual problems, the solution to which have yet to win consensus amongst philosophers. If human beings are embodied minds rather than embodied souls, how should we understand the mind and consciousness within a naturalistic framework? If ought-judgments cannot be deduced from is- statements, how can morality be justified by human experience alone? How explain the fact that theistic beliefs continue to appeal, not just to hundreds of millions of believers all over the world, but to some of the best minds in every generation? How can naturalists make sense of what William James calls "the varieties of religious experience"? If theists must wrestle with the problem of evil and the problem of the diversity of religious belief, naturalists must wrestle with the problems for which theism was often invoked. Whether you are a theist or a naturalist, your worldview is, in its global sweep, more an article of faith than a proven article.

So much for the different worldviews, but how might they affect our conception of the nature of evil and the traditional problem of evil? Theists sought an answer to the problem of evil by drawing a distinction between two kinds of evil: moral evil and natural evil. Since that perspective is useful, both in understanding the theistic position and in sketching a naturalistic alternative, I will employ it here. Roughly speaking, moral evil is evil *done* by human agents exercising their free will; natural evil is evil that *happens* to human beings as the result of moral evil or as the result of the impersonal working of the forces of nature. As Jeffrey Burton Russell puts it, "You suffer if you are struck down by a wooden beam, whether the beam is a club that I wield or a roof falling on you in the course of an earthquake."[2] Whether moral or natural, both forms of evil can involve intense, prolonged, and apparently pointless suffering, but they differ in the source of this suffering.

Moral evils for theists are sins, and sin can be thought of in either of two ways: as the violation of one of God's commandments, or as the cause of needless suffering—suffering which is neither deserved nor necessary to promote some greater good or prevent some greater evil. Though these two conceptions of sin can be distinguished, perhaps they come together if we think of God as forbidding certain actions because of their tendency to cause needless suffering. The agent of moral evil normally inflicts suffering on others, and unwittingly on himself through human or divine retribution.

Divorced from the idea of original sin for which they are punishment, natural evils are evils that afflict human beings regardless of their moral deserts. The paradigm of such evil is no doubt undeserved pain and suffering, especially when intense and prolonged, but such evils are not limited to the experience of physical pain and emotional suffering. If a rockslide kills me suddenly and painlessly, I endure a natural evil without the experience of pain or suffering; similarly, if the blow fails to kill me but renders me permanently insensible of my loss. In another sense of the term, however, I could be said to *suffers* major loss in either case, without experiencing the loss as such. Adopting a suitably broad notion of suffering, which encompasses more than the felt experience, we could perhaps accept the idea that natural evils are causes of suffering, both experiential and nonexperiential. As such, natural evils include the material effects of natural disasters (ironically referred to by insurance companies as "acts of God"), the ravages of disease and incapacitation, the deprivation of the necessities of life, and of course the prospect of death, whether sudden or lingering. Natural evils are, you might say, the shadow side of life on earth.

From the point of view of the theist, the distinction between moral and natural evil has a lot of merit. For it allows him to claim that moral evil and much of natural evil—the part which results from the effects of moral evil—is the work of man, not God. If human beings are free in a libertarian sense, it does seem as if they, and they alone, are responsible for much of the evil in the world. God could have prevented that evil by creating and manipulating human puppets who did nothing but good, but presumably that alternative would have been the lesser good. The greater good, therefore, may require real human beings to tolerate many natural evils.

What about that portion of natural evils for which human beings apparently are not responsible? As is well known, the theist can offer a variety of answers, of which I'll briefly consider and comment on four. The first two could be called the Biblical answers, for they are found in the story of Adam's fall and the story of Job's tribulations. The first suggests that the burdens of nature are the result of sin, falling not just upon the original sinners but also upon their descendants to the nth generation, and as such may be regarded as just punishment for sin.

This familiar view is often ridiculed today, but I think it has a point, in allowing for guilt of which we are not sensible. I may be robbed and beaten without ever having been guilty of those crimes myself, but perhaps I am guilty of something else, such as failing to be charitable when charity is called for. Though innocent of certain sins, I may be guilty of others, and so I may be justly punished, not for what I've done, but for what I've failed to do. However, while the idea of punishment for unrecognized sins has some plausibility, the idea of collective responsibility is more difficult to entertain. Why should the father's crime implicate the son, unless the son has tried to hide the crime or gained advantages to which he is not entitled?

The second Biblical answer to the problem of evil is found in the story of Job, in the idea that misfortune should be conceived not as punishment but as a test of faith. Perhaps the story of Abraham being called upon to sacrifice Isaac, his only son, can be interpreted along similar lines. These stories suggest two lessons, the first of which can be accepted by anybody, naturalist or theist, but the second only by a theist. The first is that adversity and misfortune can happen to the innocent and the righteous, no less than to the wicked and the unjust. The second is that good people of steadfast faith can, like Job and Abraham, ultimately gain far more than they lose. So they can, but only if the world is what theists take it to be. As long as belief is one thing and its truth another, faith in divine providence may be no more than a pious hope.

The idea of meeting tribulation with fortitude and resolve is a hard lesson, difficult for anybody to learn and often worth learning, but it has its limitations. Unlike many children and variously handicapped adults, Job and Abraham were mature and strong individuals, in a position to be tested by and to profit from adversity. As far as I know, there is nothing in the theist's story to restrict the test of adversity to those who are in a position to bear it. Without such a restriction the test is hardly fair to those who are not equipped to take it: a college-level test is appropriate for college students but not for pupils in elementary school. Isn't it gratuitous to assume that people are never "put to the test" until ready for it?

Those natural evils for which humans are not responsible can also be justified in a third way, which John Hick attributes to the second century church father St. Irenaeus and calls the Irenaean theodicy. On this view, Hick tells us God's purpose was not to construct a paradise whose inhabitants would experience a maximum of pleasure and a minimum of pain. The world is seen, instead, as a place of "soul-making" or person-making in which free beings, grappling with the tasks and challenges of their existence in a common environment, may become "children of God" and "heirs of eternal life."[3]

In short, suffering can be a means of spiritual growth. By living through his own experience of ill health, the patient can both gain a better appreciation of the blessing of health and an awakened sympathy for those who, like himself, have been forced to bear that burden.

There is, in my opinion, much wisdom in the Irenaean approach. It teaches us that, just as good fortune is not necessarily a blessing (are lottery winners the happiest of people?), so misfortune is not necessarily a tragedy (can't we be stronger for overcoming life's obstacles?) But of course it is liable to the same kind of difficulty as the test of faith approach. Recovering from serious illness, you can gain insight into the debilitating nature of illness and sympathy for the plight of the sick, but if you don't recover and your illness only gets more painful and more incapacitating, ending in death, talk about "soul-making" here can only be a joke. As Hick himself concedes, the Irenaean theodicy requires the doctrine of life after death. Theists can supply the doctrine but unfortunately not the article.

Finally, some natural evils have been justified on the ground that the suffering they involve is the result of the working of the laws of nature, or the requirement for learning about the laws of nature from experience. Because fire burns, we can use it to heat our homes and cook our food. But the nature of fire also allows it, when out of control, to burn down buildings and forests, and to cause intensely painful sensations in contact with skin. Since fire cannot do one thing without doing the other, and since we cannot learn about the nature of fire without learning about its ability to produce both kinds of effect, there is no way in which the laws of nature could have only good effects or in which we could learn about the laws of nature solely through their good effects.

I think this is a valid point about the laws of nature and the conditions which are necessary for learning about them, and no doubt it could be a reason for God's permitting a certain class of evils, if there is a God, but it should be obvious that there is a logical gap between what *could be* and what *is* the case. The naturalist, no less than the theist, can avail himself of like observations about the laws of nature without any commitment to a supernatural agency. Consequently, I think the theistic account offers a *possible* story of the nature and justification of natural evil, but that is all. Possible or "just so" stories are not to be despised, for they open our minds to unsuspected alternatives, but neither should they be received as more than they are.

The limitation of such stories is suggested by my present predicament. I have mislaid my glasses, as I've often done in the past Usually, after some searching, I find them: in the living room, the kitchen, the bathroom. But maybe this time I won't find them. Somebody may have stolen and run away with them. That is possible and, if I can't find my glasses in any of the places I normally search, I should take that possibility seriously, especially if my neighbor reports that he saw a suspicious-looking stranger at my door recently. But otherwise I shall continue to look for my glasses in the expectation that I will find them where I last left them, and treat the hypothesis that they have been stolen as a mere *possibility*— something not ruled out but, in the absence of singular information, not to be taken seriously.

There is an additional difficulty in the "just so" stories of theists who appeal to free will to resolve the problem of evil. While their strategy relieves God of responsibility for evil, it presupposes a libertarian conception of free will: the idea that human beings are free and morally responsible for their actions if and only if, under preexisting causal conditions, they could have acted otherwise. As a result, free will theism, as it might be called, is hostage to the incompatibility position on the relation between free will and causal determinism.

Two comments on this connection are in order. First, the debate over the coherence and credibility of this conception of free will is far from closed. To this extent free will theism takes a stand on an issue where the jury is, so to speak, still out. Second, unlike free will theism, naturalism is not constrained in this way. As far as naturalism is concerned, people are free when their actions spring from their own character, desires and beliefs, regardless of whether these factors could, all things considered, have been different. To this extent, naturalism is compatible with, but not committed to, universal causal determinism. It allows events, including human actions, to be causally open or closed.

To be sure, some theists are not committed to the libertarian conception of free will. As the doctrine of predestination indicates, they can countenance a form of free will which is compatible with determinism. If God predestines who is saved and who is damned, human free will is either impotent or determined by the Almighty himself. God's omnipotence is secure but the security comes at a price: it now looks as if God is the author not just of creation's good but of its evil as well. The theist is thus faced with the dilemma: libertarian free will and man's responsibility for evil, or no such commitment and the threat of God's responsibility for evil. While naturalism faces its own challenges, that is one difficulty it doesn't have to face.

So far we've discussed moral and natural evil primarily from the theistic perspective. To what extent is that distinction available to the naturalist?

My answer is: to a surprising extent, for the naturalist, no less than the theist, can exploit the distinction between what we do and what befalls us. But first I would like to enlarge on what I take to be the naturalistic stance toward suffering. While he doesn't condone the fact, the naturalist recognizes that some degree of suffering is only to be expected in a world where human beings and other creatures compete, individually and collectively, for limited resources.

Two features of this world are striking. First, the world itself— nature--is neither benign nor hostile to the creatures it contains. Its absence of hostility is shown by the fact that creatures are here at all and sometimes even manage to thrive. But nature is not benign and providential, as theists take God to be. We are here because physical conditions are right for us to be here; conditions aren't right so we can be here. Consequently, if nature provides food and water and other necessities of life, it also provides a host of tribulations that often make life not worth living. If you think of nature as a parent— Mother Nature, if you will—she seems to be an irresponsible parent. But there is no need to think of nature like that. Nature is not an individual agent like God but only a motley collection of mutually dependent creatures struggling within a physical environment that has planned neither for their presence nor for their demise. We humans, animals and plants are here and will eventually disappear— that is all. The view is bleak only if you presume that we can't be that unimportant to the universe. But nothing is important to the universe, for the universe does not have an interest or a point of view, any more than a mountain does.

The second striking feature is a fact about us. Human beings are neither angels nor devils. Not being angels, we generally prefer our own wellbeing and that of family and friends to the wellbeing of strangers, even if a small sacrifice on our part would greatly increase the wellbeing of strangers. (And most of the world consists of strangers!) Not being devils, we are capable of rising above a purely personal point of view, and of entering into and abiding by agreements with others, even strangers. I take it that the basic point of these agreements is to cooperate on terms that are to our mutual advantage. I agree to respect your life and property on condition that you respect mine. In the normal course of events, we're both gainers from this mutual restraint. But, not being angels, we're always subject to the temptation to defect, to enlarge our portion at the cost of our neighbor's, and when we succumb to this temptation, we become each other's enemies. You might say that the natural condition of humankind is Prisoner's Dilemma, writ large. For our own good we need, as a rule, to be forced to be good. In effect, that is, or should be, the role of the military, to protect us from the militaries of other nations, and also the role of the criminal justice system, to protect us from individual defectors within. Hobbes' picture of our human state is close to the truth, even if his prescription for improving that state needs to be amended.

So much then for the setting. How does evil come on the scene? It comes, as suggested before, in the form of suffering, but the sources of this suffering differ in characteristic ways. Two major sources of suffering stand out: the harmful deeds and omissions of human agents, whether through intention, negligence, inadvertence, or ignorance; and the vulnerability of human beings and other animals to a host of ills, some but not all of which are due to the nature of nature. First, there is the evil that men do. Through violence and the threat of violence, deception and exploitation, human beings are responsible for creating suffering on a massive scale—not only human suffering but, in our customary ways of dealing with nonhuman animals, their suffering as well. Genocide, enslavement, persecution and oppression are practiced against whole peoples. Crimes against persons and crimes against property are practiced against individuals and sometimes, when discrimination is present, even against whole groups. Malice masked as retribution, indifference as impartiality, and negligence as personal freedom, are as common as dirt. Is it any wonder that these practices commonly cause their victims great suffering? Is it any wonder that their victims are filled with resentment, hatred, and the lust for revenge? Those who suffer and seek redress call these practices *evil* and their doers *evildoers,* to mark them off as especially bad. Evil is worse than bad; it is bad at its worst. There is no stronger term of moral condemnation.

Since this notion of evil has ties to the theist's notion of moral evil, it can be regarded as its naturalistic counterpart. The difference between them is that, whereas the theist views moral evil as primarily an outrage against God, the naturalist views moral evil as primarily an outrage against humanity. Though the two ideas are not identical, they admit of considerable overlap, for many, if not most, of the behaviors and traits of character condemned by theism are also anathema to a humanistic form of naturalism.

The second major source of suffering rises not from what we do but from what befalls us, either because of what others do to us or because of what nature does to us, through deprivation, aging, illness, and death. In a word, we are vulnerable, which means being liable to a certain kind of harm and consequent suffering. Jones can't murder Smith unless Smith's life can be taken, and the fact that Smith's life can be taken makes him vulnerable in a special way and gives him special reason to protect himself, as far as he can, against this eventuality. Being invulnerable to bullets and speeding trains, Superman can't be harmed by either. Every living thing is liable to harm, including death, and some living things like ourselves are liable to a particularly wide range of harms before we die. While our vulnerability by itself is not a cause of suffering, it exposes us to the risk of suffering and requires us to take whatever steps we can to minimize that risk. Is it too much to suggest that our vulnerability is a *potential* for suffering?

While our vulnerability to harm is not in itself a natural evil, can it be said that, when a particular harm is realized, it becomes a natural evil? There is no doubt that, when the harm is serious and produced by human agency, the harm is of a moral nature and may be stigmatized as evil, but that wouldn't make the harm itself evil, unless we stipulate that any serious harm, however produced, is evil. Should we go so far? The question is complex and allows for more than one answer. On one hand, there are those who insist that evil intent must lie behind an evil outcome. If I intend you no harm, I do you no evil, however much harm I do you in fact. *Ipso facto,* if an earthquake wipes out your family, it harms you greatly and irreparably but it does you no evil. On this view, there may be natural harms— i.e. harms from natural sources—but there are no natural evils as distinct from moral evils.

On the other hand, we sometimes speak of evil where no intent, evil or otherwise, is involved. For example, faced by a forced choice between two unequal risks of harm, we are advised to choose the lesser evil. And the evils in question may be wholly natural, as when a physician tells his patient that she needs an operation or she will die. We are also told that the evil that men do lives after them and that evil comes to him who evil thinks. The traitor betrays his country and a train of miseries and disasters beset his countrymen for generations. The loser in a political election is filled with bitterness, turns to drink to drown his sorrows, and finally becomes an alcoholic. Examples like these suggest that we do no violence to the term in speaking of the pressing need for an operation, the miseries of future generations, and the bitterness of the sore loser as evils.

Moreover, there is another kind of case where many of us would agree that there is evil but no evil intent. A passerby spots a solitary toddler about to drown in a shallow pool but walks on unperturbed, doing nothing to rescue her or call for help. The passerby had no evil intent; he did not wish the child dead; he was simply indifferent to her welfare, though he knew that he could prevent great suffering at little or no cost to himself. In cases like this we can say not just that he harmed the child (moral evil) but that as a consequence of his failure to rescue, she and her parents suffered a great evil (natural evil). Serious unintentional harm can also come about through negligence (a careless hunter shoots and kills another hunter, the father of five, by mistake), inadvertence (a drunken driver crashes into a school bus, causing multiple injuries and deaths), or sheer ignorance (explorers unwittingly give natives blankets infected with smallpox). As Susan Neiman writes, "What counts is not what your road is paved with, but whether it leads to hell."[4]

I think a case can be made, therefore, for calling serious harm that happens to people for no fault of their own, evil. And my Webster's dictionary seems to agree, for two of the meanings it gives for "evil" are "morally corrupt; wicked" and "producing or threatening sorrow, distress, or calamity." But I have no intent to legislate here. Perhaps the truth of the matter is that we *can* speak of natural evils but are not *required* to do so. However we speak, it is clear that humans and other animals are liable to a host of harms, some from fellow humans, some from nonhuman sources. They are the counterpart of the theist's natural evils, but have for the naturalist a different significance. As we have seen, the theist struggles to fit these evils into his theocentric worldview, with mixed success. But the naturalist faces no such challenge. For him there is no need to view natural evils as the theist views them, for they are part of the fabric of life in a world Tennyson pictures as being at war with God:

> Are God and nature then at strife,
> That nature lends such evil dreams?
> So careful of the type she seems,
> So careless of the single life.

Tennyson was wrong in only one respect. Great extinction events in the history of our planet indicate that nature can be as indifferent to the type as to the single life.

In this regard I think the naturalist has the advantage over the theist, whose justifications for natural evil can easily appear to be *ad hoc*. Just as I can save the hypothesis that my glasses were stolen by a stranger by speculating that the stranger was invisible to all but the initiated, so the theist can save his hypothesis that a just God permits the righteous to suffer by speculating that suffering serves a higher purpose, albeit one which is "inscrutable" to us in our present benighted state. Are the two cases comparable? I leave the question to you.

While naturalists don't face the theist's problem of reconciling God's agency with the variety and abundance of evil in the world, perhaps they could learn something from philosophical theists who have wrestled at length with the problem of evil. My impression is that naturalists tend either to deny that evil exists, though of course they don't deny that certain actions are wrong or that certain things are bad, or they allow a place for moral evil but apparently no place for natural evil. But there is another alternative: naturalists can recognize both kinds of evil and apply them to the kinds of example found in the literature on the problem of evil. Two examples have been much discussed. In the first, a man rapes and strangles his girlfriend's five-year-old daughter; in the second, a fawn is horribly burned in a forest fire started by lightning, and after three days finally expires.[5] The fawn, of course, could have been a human infant, separated from its parents by a raging inferno. Almost everyone would agree that these events are sad and unfortunate, but are they evil?

Both cases involve significant harm, but differ in the source of the harm. We ordinarily assume that a sane, adult human being is responsible for the foreseeable consequences of his actions, so that if he intentionally causes serious harm to innocent persons, he is responsible for that harm. Because of the enormity of the harm and the innocence of the victim, the murder case qualifies as a paradigm example of moral evil. Harm, of course, can take many forms and occur in many degrees, from the relatively minor (a cigarette burn) to the intermediate (foreclosure on a home) to the major (loss of eyesight or death of a loved one). And it can affect any number of people, including the agent, family members and friends, neighbors and strangers, not to speak of nonhuman animals. And of course harm can be caused in a variety of ways—by intention, negligence, inadvertence, ignorance (culpable and nonculpable), to name but a few. Many actions that cause harm are neither evil nor even wrong (police apprehend a fugitive by shooting him in the leg), and some actions are wrong without being evil (I take an extra helping of cake, leaving none for another guest), but some actions like child-murder are so egregious that they merit the designation "evil."

The notion of moral evil is perhaps less contentious than that of natural evil, but there are similarities between a moral evil like murder and a natural disaster like a devastating forest fire. Both murder and the forest fire can cause its victims great and irreparable harm-harm which they neither deserve nor stand to benefit from in any way. Of course, there are differences too. An obvious difference is that natural disasters don't have intentions, so that the harm they cause isn't brought about intentionally or in other ways that human agents can bring about harms. If natural disasters are evils, therefore, they can't be moral evils, but that doesn't prevent them from being evils in their own way—i.e. natural evils.

Two further differences can be claimed: (1) that the child-killer is "free" in the sense that he could have acted otherwise, whereas, given the laws of nature, the forest fire could not have failed to occur; and (2) that it makes sense to say of the former "He ought not to have done it," whereas it makes no sense to say of the latter "It ought not to have occurred." These claims involve large issues—too complex to consider here—but I suggest that they are irrelevant here. Not only are they too controversial to settle anything else that is controversial, but, even if true, they would not affect the present issue. If the murder of the child is evil because it causes great and irreparable harm, as I have maintained, it is evil regardless of how it was caused, whether by the agent's free will or by a string of antecedent events over which ultimately he had no control. And if the enormity of harm is sufficient to make the murder evil, it is hard to see why the enormity of harm is not sufficient to do the same for a raging forest fire. Where harm and suffering are concerned, it seems that the murder and the forest fire are in the same boat. If so, then both must be evil or neither is. You can take your pick.

One qualification regarding intention is in order. While I have argued that something can be evil without being intended, there are such things as evil intentions. Before the era of plane hijackings and terrorism, a man planted a bomb in his wife's luggage on board an airplane, with the object of getting rid of her, collecting her life insurance, and running off with his mistress. The bomb exploded in flight and dozens of passengers were killed, along with his wife. His act was evil, if anything is, and so was the intention behind it. Suppose that, by a happy accident, the bomb failed to detonate and everybody survived the flight. The man's intention would still be evil, even if it failed to materialize, because its object was to do something that would cause great harm. Intention can be evil, therefore, without actually achieving its object.

A nagging worry remains, however. The concept of natural evil has a familiar place in the philosophy of religion, but the present account extends it in two directions: (1) by transferring it to a very different context where its applicability may be in question; and (2) by allowing it to be associated with moral evil in what may be a novel way. Since the legitimacy of these extensions may be questioned, they require at least a brief response.

(1) While it certainly doesn't follow that a theistic concept has a naturalistic application, neither does it follow that it hasn't. One big difference between the two contexts is that the theist can regard natural evils as *evils*

permitted by God, for his own purposes, and therefore susceptible to some kind of moral justification. Obviously, no such justification of natural evil is available to the naturalist. In his view bad things happen to good people, and sometimes good things happen to bad people, because people live in a universe which does not share their moral ideals or ensure the distribution of happiness in accordance with virtue. That is a big difference, indeed, but without begging the question in favor of theism, it is hard to see why it prevents the naturalist from speaking of natural evils.

(2) Theists seem to assume that the distinction between the two kinds of evil is exclusive. Moral evil is regarded as evil perpetrated by human beings, natural evil as the work of nature within the divine plan. On this view, torture with its attendant suffering is a moral evil, whereas a painful and crippling disease is a natural evil. While I agree that the disease is a natural evil and the torture a moral evil, I venture to suggest that the effect of this torture-injury to the victim and intense, prolonged pain-is a natural evil. Is this a case of counting one and the same action twice? Not necessarily, for we can distinguish what an agent does intentionally, using his body and perhaps certain implements, from the effect of what he does on another party. His doing is torturing (moral evil); the effect of his doing is another's excruciating pain (natural evil). If his victim were insensitive to pain, his action could still be described in terms of torture. The gap between deed and effect can be seen more easily where there is a significant delay between the doing—say, putting poison in a patient's waterglass—and the later but predictable effect of this doing—the patient succumbs. If the agent was deluded in thinking he was putting poison in the patient's glass, his act would still be a moral evil, even if it failed to have its desired effect. The effect, therefore, can be different from the deed, and thus allow for the presence of different kinds of evil.

Though the distinction between moral and natural evil can play a useful role in naturalism, as in theism, in real life the two forms of evil are closely related. Not only do moral evils normally bring in their train natural evils, but natural evils can give rise to conditions which promote moral evils and perhaps in some cases excuse the evils in question. Here are two examples of the first situation. (1) Jones murders Smith, an innocent man. In so doing, he commits a moral evil, as a result of which a set of natural evils happen to Smith and his family and friends: his loss of life and their consequent grief and distress. (2) On a larger scale, the socially irresponsible directors of a major corporation, indifferent to the welfare of the community, approve of clear-cutting forestry practices which, combined with heavy rain, lead to severe flooding and heavy loss of life and destruction of property. In these examples, moral evils flow into natural evils, so to speak, but we can also find cases where the reverse occurs, as the next two examples suggest.

(1) Under normal conditions, Jones would not dream of harming his neighbor Smith. But Jones and his son and Smith are adrift in a lifeboat at sea with little water or food and little hope of rescue. As hope dwindles and Smith weakens, Jones conceives the idea that dispatching Smith might save both Jones and his son, or if not Jones, at least his son. With this idea in mind Jones pushes Smith overboard. Has Jones murdered Smith? Yes, but is the murder excusable? Perhaps. Whatever the verdict, it is clear that extraordinary natural circumstances pushed Jones to this extremity. We might have done as much in his position and we don't think of ourselves as murderers.

(2) Terrorists have commandeered two passenger planes and plan to use them as flying bombs. One plane has already struck its target, with devastating results, and the second plane is nearing its announced target. The only way to prevent it reaching its target and to save thousands of lives is to shoot it down, but if it is destroyed, hundreds of innocent passengers will perish along with the terrorists. What should the authorities do: shoot the plane down and kill hundreds

of innocent people or do nothing and allow it to strike its target and kill thousands of innocent people?

In this scenario moral and natural evils seem to be intertwined. Presumably, the terrorists commit two moral evils (though both have been denied by Moslem extremists): the evil of using the planes as flying bombs and the evil of creating a situation in which society or its representatives have to choose between two horrendous acts. But the moral evil so created is a natural evil for those who must decide how to deal with it, for it is an evil thrust upon them by others, not an evil of their own making. Evils of this complexity and magnitude suggest that sometimes no good options are available. Perhaps that is the essence of tragedy, that whatever good men do, they do evil.

To conclude, both theism and naturalism allow a place for the familiar distinction between the two kinds of evil. But the two worldviews are incompatible, so at least one of them must be deeply mistaken, but which one? I know of no proof either way, though considerations of one kind or another can and have been given liberally for both. Personally, I favor the naturalistic account, on the ground of its greater simplicity, but even that modest claim has been challenged by Richard Swinburne, who argues for the greater simplicity of the "personal explanation" offered by Christian theism.[6] At the end of the day, I suspect that an element of faith enters into our best guess as to the ultimate truth.

Though many naturalists will hotly dispute this concession to the theist, there is no need to do so. For faith need take over only where the evidence is less than compelling. While the evidence for naturalism is less than compelling, surely the same is true for theism, and it may be the case that faith has less distance to travel to reach a compelling case for naturalism, than it has to reach a compelling case for theism.

Suppose Nat and Theo are betting on a horse-race. Nat, unlike Theo, consults several sources: he studies the horses and the track, talks with trainers and jockeys, calculates the odds, and finally puts his money down on the favorite, believing that it is most likely to win. Theo, on the other hand, consults only one source, the owner of a rival horse, who boasts of his horse's payback and thereby convinces Theo to bet against the favorite. We don't need to know the outcome of the race to know that, despite the element of faith and the risk of error, Nat is in the stronger evidential position, making it reasonable to believe that he will prevail. That is a matter of logic, not theology.

This analogy suggests that faith need not be blind and that different articles of faith need not stand on an equal epistemic footing. If I am right that naturalism, in our time, has become more credible than its rival, then naturalism has nothing to fear from the admission that it too involves an element of faith. Contrary to Ivan Karamazov, moral and natural evil does not require the mediation of God.

---

[1]Tussman, Joseph, "Morality without Religion," *Humanist Perspectives,* Summer 2006, #157, 23-26.
[2]*The Devil: Perceptions of Evil from Antiquity to Primitive Christianity,* Cornell U.P., 24.
[3]*Philosophy of Religion,* 45-46.
[4]*Evil in Modern Thought,* 275.
[5]William L. Rowe introduced the fawn example in his "The Problem of Evil and Some Varieties of Atheism," *American Philosophical Quarterly,* 16 (Oct. 1979), 335-341.
[6] *The Coherence of Theism,* 131-8.

Reprinted with permission, "Science and Religion: An Alternative View on an Ancient Rivalry." Open Journal of Philosophy, 2020, 10, 494-510.

SCIENCE AND RELIGION: AN ALTERNATIVE VIEW OF AN ANCIENT RIVALRY

1. Introduction

Thanks to the popular writings of the "new atheists", many people have come to think of science and religion as two monoliths between which we have to choose, or at best as two "magisteria" standing in lordly independence from one another, in the manner suggested by Stephen Jay Gould.

I will argue that both views are mistaken and spring from an impoverished understanding of their subject-matter. The conflict view treats religion as if it were identical with monotheism, but a survey of the world's major religions shows that, on the contrary, there are many religions and that they are remarkably diverse. Not all are monotheistic, or even theistic. It also suggests a simplistic view of science. While science can be said to be the study of nature, nature as a whole is too large and too complex to be the object of single-minded study. Instead, we study the significant parts of nature and in so doing create a host of highly specialized sciences, from physics to linguistics.

While Gould's view removes the conflict, it attaches to religion the idea that its exclusive concern is with values and optimizing the meaning of life. This idea is faulty on two scores. First, important as values are in religion, they have long been the concern of other disciplines, including normative ethics and moral psychology. Second, as its literature shows, religion is no less concerned with the nature of reality than it is with the nature of morality, and for understandable reasons. As Hume famously suggested in his *Treatise*, values and facts are interconnected, which renders absurd the idea of treating values as if they were a separate domain. To paraphrase a famous observation by Einstein, facts without values are lame (why should we care about the facts?), and values without facts are blind (why these values and not others?). For human life to be meaningful it is imperative to develop a coherent set of values within the constraint of the best available information about the world.

2. Religion: A Family-Resemblance Model

In thinking about religion, we want to avoid the comic mistake of the Reverend Thwackum, parodied by Henry Fielding in his novel Tom Jones. This is the fallacy of defining religion in terms that are true, at most, of one particular religion. "When I mention religion", the Reverend says, "I mean the Christian religion; and not only the Christian religion, but the Protestant religion; and not only the Protestant religion but the Church of England" (Fielding, 1749, 1980: p. 211). Ergo, religion is the Church of England. The mistake is easy to see but hard to avoid. The Church of England is a religion, not religion. Even Christianity is a religion, or, better, a set of religions and the same thing is true of Judaism and Islam. Religion cannot be defined as belief in God, for there are polytheistic religions like Hinduism and godless religions like Theraveda Buddhism. Spinoza proposed a philosophical religion, identifying God and nature as different aspects of what is essentially one, today known as pantheism. Theologian Paul Tillich spoke of religion as "faith in ultimate concern" (Tillich, 1957, 2001: p. 7).

To deal with this multitude, William Alston, writing on religion in the Encyclopedia of Philosophy (Edwards, 1967), took a cue from Wittgenstein's conception of a family resemblance term (Wittgenstein, 1953: sections 67-68).

He defined religion in terms of a cluster of nine "religion-making characteristics" which may, but need not all, be present for something to count as a religion:

> Belief in a supernatural being or beings (gods).
>
> A distinction between sacred and profane objects.
>
> Ritual acts focused on sacred objects.
>
> A moral code believed to be sanctioned by gods.
>
> Characteristically religious feelings (awe, sense of mystery, sense of guilt, adoration...connected in idea with gods).
>
> Prayer and other forms of communication with gods.
>
> A world view, or general picture of the world as a whole, including one's place in it...
>
> A more or less total organization of one's life based on this world view.
>
> A social group bound together by the above.

Far from being just a matter of belief, religion includes a cluster of other special features, including emotions, rituals, social practices, and moral codes.

No doubt there are variations here, especially between theistic religions like Christianity, which envisage divinity outside the world, and nontheistic religions like Buddhism which find divinity within the world. Whereas the former is more exemplary of religion, because they exhibit all of these features, the latter are still examples of religion, because they satisfy enough of them. The boundaries of religion are broad enough to include, not just varieties of theism, but also varieties of nontheistic religions, like Taoism and Confucianism, according to Huston Smith's well-known study (Smith, 1958).

Instead of defining religion in terms of organized religions, Ninian Smart, possibly the preeminent scholar of religious studies in English in the twentieth century, takes a different tack. In his (Smart, 1989), he proposes a seven-part "scheme of study" for the subject. It includes the practical and ritual, the experiential and emotional, the mythic or narrative ("the story side of religion"), the doctrinal and philosophical, the ethical and the legal, the social and the institutional, and the material (buildings, artifacts, etc.) As he says (p. 12),

> Though we use the singular label "Christianity," in fact there are a great many varieties of Christianity, and there are movements about which we may have doubt as to whether they count as Christian. The same is true of all traditions: they manifest themselves as a loosely held-together family of subtraditions.

The moral to be drawn from these scholars is that religions without gods are still religions, even if religions with gods are more exemplary of that category. By analogy, when people think of birds, a robin is more exemplary than a penguin or ostrich, but that doesn't mean that the latter are not birds. In *The World Until Yesterday*, Jared Diamond (2012) points out that the preoccupation with religion as a separate category is a modern development, not shared by earlier societies, which did not distinguish religion from its other activities.

Just as language is a family of languages, it is possible to think of religion as a family of religions. Where the relationship is close, as it is for some forms of Protestantism, we may prefer to speak of denominations, but the spread between Roman Catholicism and Protestantism seems to be large enough to call them separate religions. In any case, the spread between the world's major religions is wide, and that between the theistic and nontheistic varieties is even wider. The parallel with language-families like Indo-European and Sino-Tibetan comes to mind. Members of the family of religions are no less diverse than the languages they speak.

Like human families, its members are often fractious and squabble with one another in great events like the crusades and the inquisition. Some of its members even quarrel with science itself, as shown by the Church's opposition to Galileo's defense of the heliocentric theory and the creationist attack on the teaching of evolution in public schools. If you identify religion with movements like these, you will undoubtedly see religion as the enemy of science and progress. But that is the Thwackum fallacy all over again. The adherents of a particular faith may be at war with science but that doesn't mean that religion is at war with science. Indeed, many reputable scientists are self-confessed believers, as is Francis S. Collins (2006), author of *The Language of God: A Scientist Presents Evidence for Belief* as well as leader of the human genome project and later head of the NIH.

3. A New Perspective on Science

In contrast to the idea of many religions, people tend to think of science as a single- minded enterprise, pursued by a common method, and leading to uniform results. If they are sophisticated, they may realize that in fact science consists of many fields or branches: after all, the study of physics is not the same as the study of biology or psychology. But the absence of overt friction between them, apart perhaps for public funding, makes it easy to presume that they are "one." The truth, however, is more complex. Science can be regarded as a family of sciences, like the family of religions, except that its members are united by a single aim: understanding the natural world by experiential means. The common task of the sciences is to break up the study of what is given to us by nature into accessible parcels ("carving nature at the joints"). This task is often called the project of methodological naturalism: describing nature by the means that it supplies: the use of our senses and natural faculties, along with their extension by specialized instruments and the use of cognitive tools like mathematics. Despite this common aim, the study of matter is not the same as the study of living matter or the study of intelligent matter. For, while the latter studies must be consonant with the former, it does not follow that they can be reduced to it. Arguably, physics is more fundamental than biology or psychology, but the net of physics doesn't capture all the fish in the sea.

As far as vaunted scientific method goes, it can be described in very general terms as a mix of observation, measurement, proposed explanatory hypotheses, testable predictions, confirmation or its opposite, and review and replicability, but it is practiced very differently in physics than in (say) psychology. The results of these practices may require very different procedures and vocabularies, so that familiarity with one science does not guarantee familiarity with others. A person would have to be very naïve to suppose that learning about human psychology would equip him to understand the abstractions of physics. It is safe to say, however, that a psychological hypothesis that flew in the face of our best understanding of biology or physics would be, for that very reason, highly suspect.

Depending on the scope of their study, we can distinguish three major groups of scientific activity. First and foremost are the physical sciences, whose scope is the universe as a whole: physics, astronomy, cosmology, and chemistry. Astronomy and astrophysics, as their names imply, are classic examples of the broad sweep of this group of sciences. Physics endeavors to tell us about matter and energy, not just in our terrestrial environment, but anywhere in the universe. Thanks to its study of the elements, chemistry can now put to rest the complaint of Auguste Comte that man will never know the composition of the stars (Hearnshaw, 2010).

Second are those sciences which could be called earth sciences, for they focus on special features of our planet: biology, paleontology, geology, oceanography, and meteorology. While some features of our home planet are shared by other planets, we do not know whether this is true of other features, like the presence of intelligent life. Despite SETI—the search for extraterrestrial intelligent life—intelligent life could be a unique feature of Earth. This seems to have been Pascal's view of man: "Man is only a reed, the weakest thing in nature; but he is a thinking reed". Pascal took for granted that this reed was alone in the universe. In contrast, many scientists now take panspermia and the evolutionary process for granted: given the right natural conditions, simple living organisms will emerge and, with sufficient time, evolve into complex varieties of life.

Third is that cluster of sciences which, for want of a better name, we could call the human sciences because they focus on our species: anthropology, archaeology, sociology, psychology, economics, and linguistics. The narrow but richly detailed focus of the human sciences contrasts with the broad but less intimate focus of the physical sciences, in a way that invites the analogy between the map of a city (the human sciences) and the two-dimensional map of the globe (the physical sciences). Changes of scale bring new worlds into view. For physics, fair reader, you are just another hunk of matter; for chemistry, a bag of chemicals; for biology, an animal of the species Homo sapiens ; for psychology, a male or female of a certain age and profile. Each level hives off certain features, the objects of its special attention, and ignores others, which figure only in the background. The scope of our subject shrinks as we narrow our field of view, but at the same time, it brings to light new phenomena in greater depth and richness of detail.

Two objections to this sketch are worth addressing. First, as already noted, we often speak of fields or branches of science rather than of multiple sciences. True, speaking of fields or branches may reduce the impression of diversity, but the diversity is there. The study of the physical sciences is very different from what I call the human sciences; some scientists even question whether the latter are genuine sciences. We have a situation analogous to that of religion. Some people but not others are inclined to deny that nontheistic religions are truly religions, just as some deny that psychology is truly a science.

The issue should not be decided by fiat. As Charles Darwin (Darwin, 1857) suggested, there are alternative ways of describing the same class of things. Splitters prefer a narrower, lumpers a broader, conception of a subject-matter. What is a matter of choice allows either party to speak as they choose. The important thing is to understand, not to legislate, usage. I see no harm in speaking of psychology as a science, as long as we bear in mind that its subject-matter and its application of scientific method are different in scope and detail from that of physics but suitable for its own type of investigation. The same point goes for the larger topic of science itself. Impressed by its methodological naturalism, we may be tempted to think of it as a monolith, but at the same time, we should never overlook the diversity of its broad subject matter—a perspective which enables us to view science as a family of sciences. That does not mean it is wrong to speak of science in the singular (e.g., "science today was once known as natural philosophy"), where the intended reference is all recognized sciences, any more than it is wrong to speak of language in the singular, when the intended reference is all recognized human languages.

The second objection has to do with the delineation of the sciences. Astronomy by all accounts is a science, but is cosmology, the study of the history of the universe, a separate science or only a branch of astronomy? A similar question can be asked about anthropology and archeology. I hold no brief on questions of this sort, important as they are for many specialists. While there is room on my provisional list for additions and/or deletions, there clearly is a difference between the study of features of the universe as a whole and the study of its focal parts. Given this difference, it is not surprising that mathematics plays a major role in the physical sciences but less so in those sciences which call for intensive field investigation.

The plurality of sciences resembles the plurality of religions, but there are three important differences. First, the family of sciences is compatible with each other in a way that is not true of the family of religions. At crucial points Christianity wars with Islam and Buddhism, but astronomy does not war with biology or sociology. The sciences can be represented on a three-tiered pyramid, with physical sciences on the bottom, human sciences on the top, and earth sciences in the middle. Their mutual coherence helps to explain why people tend to see the sciences as one and to repose greater confidence in them than in religion. As far as I can see, no such pyramid is possible for the world's major religions. We can think of the family of sciences as exhibiting unity in diversity, unlike the family of religions which notoriously exhibit diversity without unity.

Second, there is the matter of methodology. While science is associated with the scientific method, there is no such thing as the "religious method." Believers often speak of "faith" but it is often faith in the deliverances of one or more informal ways of supporting belief. These ways include revelation (testimony as to God's word); historical evidence (fulfillment of prophecies and performance of miracles); religious experience (the experience of conversion and feelings of awe and dependence); the need for morality (allegedly absent in a godless world); and reason (the argument from design and many others). This is merely a sketch, and it takes no stand on whether any of these ways can properly be called methods. The point is not that religion has its own methods, but that religious beliefs have been, and are, backed up in ways that for the most part are foreign to scientific practice.

Finally, there is the question of moral guidance. Traditionally, this task has fallen to the lot of religion and sometimes to moral philosophy, but not to science. Scientists offer no injunctions of the form "Thou shalt not take human life", not because they are, as human beings, indifferent to morality, but because their field of expertise gives them no special insight into this domain. Behavioral scientists can, of course, study the behavior of people who violate social norms, offer hypotheses about the causes of such behavior and its typical outcomes ("crime doesn't pay"), but it is not their job, as scientists, to offer moral instruction. If an eminent scientist were to proclaim on TV, "Taking innocent human life is wrong", he would be understood by viewers as expressing his private moral convictions, not as an expert on morality. (Are there such experts?) Yes, people sometimes make use of science to give weight to their moral pronouncements—" Science says that smoking is bad for you"—but science itself is not in the business of telling people what to do. As far as science goes, you can smoke if immediate gratification means more to you at this time than its long-term health impact (Hempel, 1988: pp. 334-348).

Science, as sketched above, needs to be distinguished from two adjacent areas: technology and mathematics. Technology can be regarded as the application of basic scientific knowledge to serve human ends, which range across the board from life-saving measures to weapons of mass destruction. To some thinkers, technology holds the promise of utopia, including the abolition of suffering and the inevitability of death, and to others, it threatens the survival of our species. Technology is the business end of science, and advances in technology help to explain why science is popular with the public. Many people see no need to distinguish between science and technology but surely there is a difference between knowing that water expands when it freezes and knowing how to build a refrigerator. People have known the former since ancient times, but no one knew how to do the latter until the nineteenth century.

Mathematics, on the other hand, is another story. While it is valued as an essential tool in scientific practice, it has long been known to be an independent science, based on a priori reflection rather than empirical investigation and discovery. For example, once we learn that any number can be increased by the addition of one, we can easily infer that the number of numbers must be infinite. It would be naïve to suppose that we discover this fact by the use of scientific method. The distinction between pure and applied math is apt. The former is an independent discipline, the latter a handmaid to the sciences.

It should be clear by now how science and religion are similar in some respects but not in others. Given these complex relations, it makes no sense to say that they are friends or foes. Religion as such is not incompatible with science, though some religions are, and many religions are incompatible with each other. There are religious wars but no science wars in which a recognized science X wars with another recognized science Y, though of course there are disputes about science matters and real wars that make use of science. Einstein, who had much to say about both domains, seemed to think that science and religion were complementary. "Science without religion is lame", he observed, "religion without science is blind" (Einstein, 1941). Einstein may have looked to religion for something he could not find in science—moral guidance.

4. Science and the New Atheism

The new atheists—usually identified as evolutionist Richard Dawkins (2006), neurologist Sam Harris (2004), journalist Christopher Hitchens (2007), and philosopher Daniel Dennett (2006)—have each written full-length works in which they take for granted that science and religion are in conflict. As they see it, religion is faith-based belief in the primacy of the supernatural realm, whereas science is evidence-based belief in the only world there is—the natural world. Given their assumptions, it is hard to quarrel with their conclusion, but there is no need to make such a gift, for their assumptions are highly questionable.

The new atheists speak of religion as if were identical with theism: belief in one or more supernatural beings who bear a superficial resemblance to human beings but vastly exceed them in power, knowledge, and benevolence or malevolence. While it is true that many people think of religion in those terms, a broad view of religion, such as we find in Alston and other scholars, does not support this outlook. To fail to see that religion can take non-theistic forms is another manifestation of the Reverend Thwackum fallacy. Despite his prominence as a Christian philosopher, Alston found it necessary, as we have seen, to endorse an approach to religion that did not tie it to the apron strings of theism. Ninian Smart (1989) and Huston Smith (1958) are other scholars who separate the study of religion from the study of theology and celebrate the diversity and plurality of religious traditions. That is not to deny the possibility of stipulating that nothing counts as a religion unless it involves belief in a supreme being, but, as Bertrand Russell said (Russell, 2019): "The method of 'postulating' what we want has many advantages: they are the same as the advantages of theft over honest toil."

Is it true that religion, unlike science, is no more than faith-based belief? No doubt faith plays a more prominent role in religion than in science, but, as we already noted, it can take the form of faith in a variety of sources, including some that are not confined to religion, like history, reason, and experience. In my view, none of these sources yield unequivocal support for theistic belief. But it is tendentious to imply, as atheists often do, that theists draw no distinction between blind faith and faith that looks for support outside the individual's state of mind. Evidence-based as it is, it is doubtful whether science itself can altogether escape some element of faith: apart from "animal faith" (Santayana, 1923, 1955), can you be sure that the pursuit of science will work as well in the future as it has worked in the past? The problem of induction aside, what if it led to nuclear war or Greenhouse Earth and the demise of civilization?

In their opposition to religion, the new atheists seem to take for granted that the only things which exist and of which knowledge is possible are the objects within the purview of science. Call these natural objects. Since gods, demons, souls, and their like are not natural objects, it follows therefrom that they cannot exist and that, while belief in them is possible, none of it can rise to the level of knowledge. Embedded in this position, therefore, are profound negative metaphysical and epistemological implications, to the effect that "Nature is all there is", a doctrine known as "metaphysical naturalism" or colloquially as "scientism".

I would like to make two points about scientism. First, as far as I can see, scientism may well be true. Science has made great strides in explaining a wide variety of natural phenomena, some of which had long evaded its grasp. Meanwhile, the opponents of scientism continue to quarrel amongst themselves, without any end in sight. In some cases, the absence of probative evidence for something is evidence of its absence, and this may be one of them. Whether scientism is true, however, is not the point. The point is whether science, as we know it today, entitles us to draw such sweeping conclusions. That case remains to be made.

My second point is that scientism is not the same as methodological naturalism, the framework of science. The latter counsels scientists to investigate nature by natural (i.e., experiential) means. It does not counsel them to ignore anything that cannot be investigated in this way. Mathematics is the striking example of a discipline which floats free from the tribunal of experience. If one discipline can escape this taskmaster, there is no a priori reason why it alone can do so.

While this point is often overlooked, mathematics like philosophy is another arm-chair discipline. Only those who do not engage fully with these subjects would condemn them for that reason. At high levels of abstraction mind-work can be no less demanding than experimental work in the lab or investigative work in the field. While it nowhere achieves the rigor and consensus amongst its practitioners as is found in math, philosophy can be described as a discipline whose practitioners aspire to the a priori status of mathematics.

This aspiration is exemplified in the Cartesian program (Descartes, 1641, 1984a) to reform the structure of human knowledge on the basis of the cogito and the conjecture that God is no deceiver. Yes, the failure of that program casts doubt on the project, but another in the twentieth century might take its place— the analysis of the fundamental concepts that occur repeatedly in science, philosophy, and common life, like "causation", "law of nature", "truth", "knowledge", "mind", "free will", and the like. As yet a work in progress, conceptual studies await a final verdict. In the meantime, it appears that concepts, numbers, and other intellectual products are abstract objects and not natural ones. The relation between the abstract and the a priori calls for further investigation, beyond the bounds of this paper.

History in its various forms is another discipline where scientism may come up short. As a record of particular persons and events in the past, it is questionable whether that record can, even in principle, be derived from the general form of the laws of nature. For example, we know a great deal about the life of a particular statesman—say, Winston Churchill—but how could that knowledge be derived in its countless details from nothing but the sciences? If the other sciences cannot be reduced to physics, we should not be surprised to find that history cannot be reduced to science either.

Two further reasons can be given for highlighting the distinctive role of history. First, history is notoriously vulnerable to diverse interpretations of the events it records. Japanese and American historians can be expected to offer very different accounts of the Second World War, without either departing radically from the facts. Since the sciences themselves have their own individual histories of development—the physical sciences were the first to break away from natural philosophy—they cannot dispense with their place in the record of the past. No doubt science can have a role in historical investigation—if nobody can be raised from the dead, then the story of the revival of Lazarus must be a myth—but that is not sufficient to make history a science. Compare: scientific investigation has a role to play in verifying the authenticity of works of art, but that doesn't make art a science.

Finally, historical events are in large measure subject to contingency or chance. Events that are very probable do not always occur, and the improbable occurs instead. No better example can be found than the tragic one of Claus von Stauffenberg (Shirer, 1960: p. 1027ff.). Stauffenberg was a German army officer who on July 20, 1944 attempted to assassinate Hitler by placing a time bomb hidden in a briefcase near his feet. The bomb exploded but, improbably, Hitler survived with only minor injuries, and the Nazi party continued in power until the following year. But Stauffenberg and many others judged to be complicit in the crime were executed. Whether we expect it or not, history can take strange turns. Who could have predicted the assassination of President John F. Kennedy on November 22, 1963? Science, no less than the man on the street, is often blind to the course of events.

Since history is not a science, it is hard to see how scientism can accomplish its ambitious goal. While it aspires to speak with the authority of science, it makes commitments that are more philosophical than scientific. Science is committed to no more than methodological naturalism. This form of naturalism is committed to the reality of the natural world and our access to it, without insisting that nature, as depicted by science today, is all there is. As Hamlet tells Horatio, "There are more things in heaven and earth/Than are dreamt of in your philosophy." Scientists have confirmed this observation many times in the last hundred years. Who would have guessed that there are billions of galaxies beyond the Milky Way, that black holes are found at the center of galaxies, that the universe itself began in a kind of violent explosion?

As for the new atheists, they would do well to rest content with the virtues of methodological naturalism and to temper their animosity to religion. Even if a supernatural being is not needed to explain the wonders of astronomy, as Laplace is reported to have said to Napoleon, the idea of a God who favors Roman Catholics and creates the world *ex nihilo* is not the whole story. Human beings have crafted a multitude of other ideas about the divine and it doesn't follow that none of these ideas has a footing in reality. For this reason, if no other, we can speculate that Hume's "wise man"—one who proportions belief to the evidence (Hume, 1748: p. 653)-- would have little use for doctrinaire forms of theism or atheism (Andre, 1993: pp. 141-142).

5. NOMA to the Rescue?

In one of his last works, *Rocks of Ages: Science and Religion in the Fullness of Life* (1999) Stephen Jay Gould proposes an alternative to the conflict model. He says that science studies the age of rocks and religion the rock of ages (p. 6). This of course is a metaphor but he unpacks it with an interesting claim. Borrowing the theological concept of a "magisterium"—a self-standing discipline which has its own problems and ways of dealing with them—Gould claims that science and religion are independent magisteria. The job of science is, by means of scientific method, to discover what is true of the natural world, and the job of religion is, by its own means, to articulate and defend those values in terms of which human beings can lead meaningful lives. He calls this principle NOMA (p. 5), short for "Non-Overlapping Magisteria." (Not to be confused with the similar sounding "majesteria").

This is an interesting proposal that is not without merit. It was anticipated by Galileo, whom Gould quotes, who said that astronomy teaches us about the heavens but religion teaches us how to get to heaven. Asked why heavy airplanes are capable of flight, it would be natural to turn to science; asked why we should not return injury for injury, it would be equally natural to say "It says so in the Gospels" or "Two wrongs don't make a right" or "An eye for an eye makes the whole world blind". In Gould's view, science deals with facts, religion with values.

But this view of science and religion is overly simplistic. The pursuit of science has its own values—coherence, reliability, simplicity, fruitfulness, etc. We could account for a miracle as the intervention of the divine spirit in the regular cycles of human life, but, as Hume argued in his essay on miracles (Hume, 1748), it is more probable that the report of a miracle is the result of mistake or deception, than that someone has witnessed the violation of a long-attested law of nature. The argument is controversial but it reflects a model of scientific thinking: this hypothesis is more probable than that one, so the wise man will accord the first greater credibility, until a better one comes along. Hume could also have said that his hypothesis is the simpler of the two, for it needs no ad hoc assumption about divine intervention. The emphasis on probability, simplicity, and the willingness to revise one's judgments in the light of new evidence is characteristic of science. Values are present in this model of thinking about the facts. Other things equal, we generally prefer the more probable or simpler hypothesis as more likely to be true. Once having settled on a hypothesis we could hold on to it come what may, but instead we prefer to revise or abandon it in the face of clear counterevidence.

If epistemic values play a role in our conception of facts, facts also play a role in our conception of values. If people turn to the Gospels for insight, it is because they see something special there: the word of God, psychological insight into human reactions, the distillation of common experience, or what have you. The idea of not returning evil for evil is so surprising to many people that they naturally ask "Why not?" As we have seen, a variety of reasons can be offered in reply, but they all purport to be relevant and factual. The reply "I have no reason" or "I just think so" or "Timbuktu is in Africa" would be unintelligible.

Paradoxically, Gould assigns to religion a task that is commonly assigned to philosophy today: the task of identifying good and evil, right and wrong, duties and rights, and other normative questions. However, in earlier times one of the central tasks of religion was to act as a moral guide, policeman, and judge. The promise of heaven and the threat of hell were held out as inducements to proper behavior. Even today millions of believers take these inducements seriously enough not only to govern their behavior, but to impose its rules on others. Secular minds may scoff at such notions as medieval superstition, but if they do, that is only because they no longer take it seriously.

Though religion has often been regarded as the guardian of public morality, when we look at the history of many religions, it is not clear that it deserves that title. Differences of religious belief and practice have often been associated with discrimination, persecution, violence, terrorism, and war. As Steven Weinberg said, "With or without religion, good people can behave well and bad people can do evil; but for good people to do evil—that takes religion" (Weinberg, 1999, 2001: p. 242). It is surprising that, in placing religion on a level with science, Gould has little to say about the dark side of the history of religion. While acknowledging that men have done evil in the name of organized religion, he dismisses further discussion of the point by attributing such evil, not to religion, but to the confluence of religion with secular power (Gould, 1999: p. 9). He does not consider the possibility that, in reposing so much confidence in faith, religion encourages its followers to exalt their faith over that of others. The exclusivism of organized religion is surely a serious matter.

Gould is right to recognize the equal importance of facts and values, but, in assigning them to different magisteria, he leaves it unclear how they can work together. And they must work together, as Hume suggests, for values are justified by their connection to facts (Hume, 1739-1740, 2006). For example, when a teacher admonishes his students "You ought to work harder" (value), he takes for granted, and hopes they will too, that working harder is in their long-term interest (fact), and that they ought to pursue what is in their long-term interest (value). A similar view of Hume's contribution has been supported by Ronald Dworkin (2011), philosopher of jurisprudence, in his recent book, *Justice for Hedgehogs.*

When the reasoning is fully spelled out, notice that the fact is sandwiched between a pair of related values, the implicit one being usually more general than the stated one, in a form of logic known as the enthymeme. Being implicit, the unstated premise is easily missed or taken for granted in a simplified form, This is unfortunate, for the implicit premise may be subject to recognized exceptions. For example, when parents counsel their youngster, "You ought not to lie, because if you do, you'll never be trusted", they may have in mind, not the unqualified "It is always wrong to lie", but something more thoughtful, like "It is always wrong to lie, except where telling the truth would cause people more harm than good".

It is true that there is no unique principle of practical deliberation. Since enthymemes can often be completed in more than one way and still be valid, this openness to interpretation may be one reason for the supply of divergent moral principles on offer. Ethics, like religion, has its own problems with competing intuitions.

While Hume's after-thought about the "is/ought" transition is hardly the last word on the subject, it does suggest that the contrast between values and facts is overdrawn. Take away the values and the fact, if that is what it is, loses its interest. The idea that facts reside in one sphere and values in another would have struck Hume as absurd.

To sum up this assessment of NOMA, Gould was right to think that the task of religion included engaging with values, but wrong to think that this was its only task or its proprietary one. This task belongs not just to religion but to philosophy and psychology, as Jonathan Haidt's (2013) *The Righteous Mind: Why Good People are Divided by Politics and Religion* amply demonstrates. Gould has given us no reason to think that religion can do it better.

The positive message of NOMA is that science and religion are not enemies between which we have to choose. Yes, there are some members of the family of religions who turn their back on science in favor of their own teachings, but equally there are other members who see no such conflict. The problem with religion is not its relation to science, but the conflict between the followers of one religion and the followers of another. A familiar example is the status of Jesus Christ. While the Christian tradition reveres him as God Incarnate or the son of God, Moslems regard him as only one of the prophets, and neither the latest nor the greatest, and Jews see him as a tragic figure within their own fold. Surely these different views can't all be true, but it is hard to see how the family of religions has the resources to sort out such conflicts, or the readiness to turn the issue over to a third party. For all practical purposes, the issue is intractable.

Theologians and philosophers of religion are aware of the problem of conflicting truth-claims, of course, but it is doubtful whether they have a good solution. John Hick, who repeatedly returned to the problem, outlines three possible approaches: exclusivism, inclusivism, and pluralism (Hick, 1963). The exclusivist favors his own religion: any competitor must be a false religion. The inclusivist may favor his own religious faith but he is prepared to grant the same privilege to followers of other faiths, like the native speaker who prefers his own language but admits that native speakers of other languages are entitled to the same privilege with regard to their own. The pluralist tends to regard existing religions as historical and cultural expressions of a transcendent reality: different names, you might say, for the same God.

None of these positions solves the problem. Exclusivists can be found in every religious tradition, refreshing the conflict, not resolving it. Inclusivism tends to collapse into relativism: the faith of culture X is true for members of X, just as the faith of culture Y is true for members of Y, regardless of whether these faiths are compatible. In doing so, the relativist conflates "true for X" with "accepted as true by X", which are not the same. Columbus accepted as true the belief that he could reach the Indies directly by sailing west, but his belief was not true. Two continents stood in his way.

The pluralist is for high-minded folks, who look on religion differently than do their low-minded brethren who take their gods for the real thing, not its simulacra. It is easier to worship Jesus as God Incarnate than as Jesus the stand-in for a God beyond reach. Hick has done a service by high-lighting different attitudes toward religion, but strangely he seems to leave out of account another trinity—skepticism, indifference, and hostility. Nevertheless, his magnum opus, *An Interpretation of Religion* (Hick, 1989), is a refined and eloquent statement of his late account of pluralism.

6. Conclusion

Familiar as disagreement and controversy are in religion, they are not absent from science either, as demonstrated by the history of science. Such disagreement can be found even in current science. For example, while the theory of evolution is at the heart of modern biology, biologists sometimes disagree about the details of how evolution works. Stephen Jay Gould himself proposed a theory of punctuated equilibrium, according to which evolution proceeds by periods of relative stability which are disrupted by cataclysmic events like the asteroid which struck the earth about sixty-five million years ago, bringing about the end of the age of dinosaurs and the beginning of the ascendancy of mammals. Gould also proposed that some features of organisms living today, like language and art, are "spandrels"—incidental features like the pictures between the arches of a cathedral—rather than the result of adaptations, in contrast to other evolutionists who continue to emphasize the adaptive value of such features.

Despite this kind of disagreement, however, the history of science gives us no reason to think that such disagreements are intractable. The readiness of scientists to look for new evidence, to put accepted theories to test, to amend or abandon them if necessary, to seek consensus by reviewing each other's results, acts over time as a brake to the development of intractable disagreement at a fundamental level. This is the respect in which science seems most different from religion. Scientists have developed a discipline which allows for disagreement and its eventual resolution, whereas their counterparts in religion—theologians—have yet to develop a discipline which allows for the resolution of fundamental disagreement. Recognizing the shortcomings of human cognitive abilities and the need for safeguards, science is prepared to be self-correcting in a way that religion is not. That may be the principal difference between the two magisteria.

References

Andre, S. (1993). "Was Hume an Atheist?" *Hume Studies*, XIX, No. 1.

Collins, F. S. (2006). *The Language of God: A Scientist Presents Evidence for Belief.* New York: Free Press.

Darwin, C. (1857) Darwin on Splitters and Lumpers. Letter to Joseph Dalton Hooker in 1857.

Dawkins, R. (2006). *The God Delusion*. Boston, MA: Houghton Mifflin.

Dennett, D. (2006). *Breaking the Spell: Religion as a Natural Phenomenon*. New York: Penguin Books.

Descartes, R. (1641, 1984a). *Meditations on First Philosophy*. In J. Cottingham, et al. (Eds.), *The Philosophical Writings of Rene Descartes* (Vol. I, pp. 111-151). Cambridge: Cambridge University Press.

Diamond, J. (2012). *What Can We Learn from Traditional Societies?* (p. 340). New York: Viking Press.

Dworkin, R. (2011). *Justice for Hedgehogs* . Boston, MA: Belknap Press of Harvard University.

Edwards, P. (1967). *The Encyclopedia of Philosophy* (8 vols. in 4). New York: Macmillan.

Einstein, A. (1941). "Religion and Science." A Symposium Published by the Conference on Science, Philosophy and Religion in their Relation to the Democratic Way of Life, Inc., New York: The Symposium.

Fielding, H. (1749, 1980). *Oxford Dictionary of Quotations* (3rd ed.) Oxford: Oxford University Press.

Gould, S. J. (1999). *Rocks of Ages: Science and Religion in the Fullness of Life*. New York: Ballantine Publishing Group.

Haidt, J. (2013). *The Righteous Mind: Why Good People Are Divided by Politics and Religion*. New York: Vintage Books.

Harris, S. (2004). *The End of Faith: Religion, Terror, and the Future of Reason*. New York: Norton.

Hearnshaw, J. B. (2010). Auguste Comte's Blunder: An Account of the First Century of Stellar Spectroscopy and How It Took One Hundred Years to Prove That Comte Was Wrong .

Hempel, C. G. (1988). "Science and Human Values." In E. D. Klemke, R. Hollinger, & A. D. Kline (Eds., Revised Ed.), *Introductory Readings in the Philosophy of Science* (pp. 334-348). Buffalo: Prometheus Books.

Hick, J. (1963). *Philosophy of Religion.* London: Prentice-Hall.

Hick, J. (1989). *An Interpretation of Religion.* Newhaven, CT: Yale University Press.

Hitchens, C. (2007). *God Is Not Great: How Religion Poisons Everything* . New York: Hatchette Book Group.

Hume, D. (1739-1740, 2006). *A Treatise of Human Nature* . Ed. with Intro by Ernest C. Mosner. London: Penguin Books.

Hume, D. (1748). *An Enquiry Concerning the Human Understanding.* In E. A. Burtt (Ed.), *The English Philosophers from Bacon to Mill.* The Modern Library. New York: Random House.

Russell, B. (2019). Logical Constructions . *Stanford Encyclopedia of Philosophy.* https://plato.stanford.edu/entries/logical-construction/

Santayana, G. (1923, 1955). *Scepticism and Animal Faith* . New York: Dover Publications.

Shirer, W. (1960). *The Rise and Fall of the Third Reich* . New York: Simon & Schuster.

Smart, N. (1989). *The World's Religions* . Cambridge: Cambridge University Press.

Smith, H. (1958). *The Religions of Man.* Reissued with Changes as *The World's Religions*, 1991. New York: Barnes & Noble.

Tillich, P. (1957, 2001). *Dynamics of Faith.* New York: Harper Collins.

Weinberg, S. (1999, 2001)."A Designer Universe?" In *Facing Up: Science and Its Cultural Adversaries* (pp. 230-242). Cambridge: Harvard University Press.

Wittgenstein, L. (1953). *Philosophical Investigations* (3rd ed., G. E. M. Anscombe, Trans.). New York: Macmillan.

Reprinted with permission, "The Problem with the Problem of Evil." Open Journal of Philosophy, 2021, 11, 336-354.

THE PROBLEM WITH THE PROBLEM OF EVIL

1. Introduction

The problem of evil has been around for a long time. It is usually posed in terms of extreme suffering, especially if intense and prolonged, regardless of whether it is physical pain, like a burn or crushing blow, or emotional distress, like grief or gripping fear. Hume attributed his version of the problem of evil to Epicurus, a Greek philosopher who lived about the third century BCE. While that attribution is doubtful, for his argument cannot be found in the few extant works of Epicurus, Hume may have made use of it for rhetorical effect or attributed it to another to spare himself the risk of being seen as an outright atheist.

There can be no doubt, however, that St. Augustine (Sparrow, 1947) in the fifth century was already aware of the problem of evil, for he developed two doctrines—the sinfulness of man and the free will defense –to deal with it. According to Augustine, God endowed man with a special gift—the gift of freedom. Unlike other animals, which were guided by instinct, man was free to obey or disobey God's instructions. God forbad Adam and Eve to eat of the tree of knowledge, but tempted by the serpent—a metaphor perhaps for their curiosity—they disobeyed God and as a result, they and their progeny were expelled from paradise. Augustine saw suffering as the result of sin, sin as the result of turning away from God, and God of course as all-powerful, all-knowing, and all-good. These ideas are still popular with believers today, though they may give less weight to the ideas of original sin and hell than did their famous predecessor.

Leibniz (*Theodicy*, 1710), the great German philosopher and polymath of the seventeenth century, who was a contemporary of Newton and vied with him over the invention of the calculus, coined the term "theodicy" from the Greek words for justice and God, "to justify the ways of God to man." He was the first to suggest the greater good defense in conjunction with the free will defense: some goods with a smidgeon of bad are better than the same goods without that smidgeon. He compared two generals with illustrious careers, one who is battle-scarred and the other who has won his battles without the scars. Leibniz thought it obvious that the battle-scarred general was more worthy. We don't have to agree with him, but Leibniz had an important insight and he took advantage of it.

Perhaps the world is better with some evil in it than it would be without any evil. It's true that a world without sentient beings like humans and other animals might be devoid of suffering, but wouldn't it be inferior to a world like our own where there are multitudes of sentient beings and, yes, some suffering but also glorious delights? That is why Leibniz maintained that this is the best of all possible worlds, not because it was free of suffering, but because it offered no more suffering than was necessary for the great good it permitted—human freedom. That is why he called this the best of all possible worlds—the kind of world you would expect God, the greatest possible being, to create.

Hume (*Dialogues Concerning Natural Religion*, 1779) may have been the first major philosopher in the modern period to make explicit use of the problem of evil to challenge the kind of theism Leibniz represented. Here are the premises of his argument (in my own words):

If God is omnipotent, he is able to eliminate evil;

If God is wholly good, he wants to prevent evil;

If God is both omnipotent and wholly good, there is no evil;

But there is evil.

From these premises it follows, not that there is no God, but that God is limited either in power or in goodness. For Christians, that was tantamount to denying the existence of God, for they regarded God as unlimited in power, wisdom, and goodness. As a result, Hume is often considered to be an atheist. But, as I and others have argued, that does not mean that Hume was a positive atheist—one who believes that there is no God. While Hume was no theist in the Christian sense, perhaps it is best to characterize him as a limited theist (Andre, 1993) or as a religious skeptic. (As scholars remind us, all of us are skeptics about the existence of some gods, like Baal and Zeus and Thor. The religious skeptic ups the ante by having doubts about the existence of any god, but he hesitates to *deny* their existence outright. Why give any hostages to fortune?) In an age when religious skepticism was not distinguished from atheism, Hume, concerned about his hard-earned literary reputation, left one of his greatest works, *Dialogues Concerning Natural Religion*, to be published only after his death. Even then, in the epilogue he saw fit to hide his religious doubts by allowing Pamphilus, the narrator of the *Dialogues*, to award the palm of victory to Demea, the conventional theist and least perspicuous character in the work. (*Dialogues*, Part XII)

Voltaire, roughly a contemporary of Hume, used literature, not philosophy, to pillory Leibniz's best of all possible worlds. Though Voltaire was no friend of organized religion, he was no atheist; as he said, "If God did not exist, it would be necessary to invent him." After the Lisbon earthquake of 1755, which killed more than 50,000 people, many of them churchgoers, as it occurred on a Sunday morning, Voltaire wrote *Candide* to mock Leibniz' ideas. As is well-known, *Candide* is the story of an absurd hero who always expects the best but ends up with the opposite. In the end, it is a good thing for him to limit himself to tending his garden.

The Reverend William Paley (1802) ignored Hume's critique of the argument from design and his version of the problem of evil. Indeed, Paley supported the idea of design with a famous analogy about the complexity of a watch and that of (say) the eye, which became the *locus classicus* of the design argument, the one likely to appear in selected readings on religion. Support for the idea of design did not change significantly until Charles Darwin published *On the Origin of Species* in 1859. As is well- known, Darwin's theory of natural selection offered a science-based alternative to the theological theory of the Designer- in- Chief. Ironically, though Darwin had begun his career as a devotee of Paley's approach, before the century was over he set it aside in favor of a more naturalistic approach. Though the death of his favorite daughter Annie may have disposed him to question the benevolence of God, it led Darwin, not to endorse the problem of evil and outright atheism, but to agnosticism (Darwin Correspondence Project, Letter to John Fordyce, 7 May 1879.)

Despite the longevity of the problem of evil, it remains contested ground today, hundreds if not thousands of years later. The battle between theists and atheists, believers and nonbelievers, rages on for readers' minds, as a glance at philosophy journals and booklists will confirm. An enquirer might well ask: What is the state of play today? Are we in the twenty-first century any nearer a consensus as to which side is gaining ground over the other, than people were in the eighteenth century? Given the volume of literature on the subject and the subtlety of many of its authors, that would be an impossible undertaking for anything short of a book. To make it possible within the compass of an article, I propose to concentrate on two leading figures in the field, William Rowe, a self-confessed atheist and inventor of a new brand he calls "friendly atheism", and

Alvin Plantinga, who has not only single-handedly revived interest in theism but also inspired others to band together under the banner of "skeptical theism."

While I don't pretend that friendly atheism and skeptical theism are the last word on the problem of evil, I believe that Rowe and Plantinga have advanced our thinking on the subject beyond that of Hume and Leibniz, and hence warrant fresh attention. That advance may encourage some of us to think that we are drawing closer to a definitive outcome than was the case before, but I will argue for three conclusions: (1) that Rowe's famous example of the burned fawn fails to make a compelling case for pointless suffering; (2) that Plantinga's "possibilities" have no cash value and that his version of the free will defense is as controversial as other forms of libertarianism; and (3) that, despite some advance on refining the problem of evil, it is time to turn from the theological issue of pointless suffering, over which progress toward consensus seems deadlocked, to consider a more mundane but plausible alternative.

2. Are God and evil Incompatible?

In the twentieth century the problem of evil developed into two versions, commonly called the logical version and the evidential version. The distinction is important, for many philosophers, believers as well as nonbelievers, are prepared to admit that the logical version of the problem of evil is now closed, whereas the evidential version is still open. This is one area where one can point to progress in dealing with the generic problem of the problem of evil.

On the face of it, there is something odd in the conjunction of God and evil. How can the world-creator who is supremely good and powerful co-exist with something whose non-existence would make the universe better off? Sensing the tension between the idea of God and the idea of evil, many people found it easy to conclude that God and evil are incompatible, so that the reality of one excludes the reality of the other. There are two ways of dealing with the alleged incompatibility. The first is to deny the reality of evil, as we find in Alexander Pope's poem *Essay on Man*:

> All nature is art unknown to thee;
> All chance, direction which thou canst not see;
> All discard, harmony not understood;
> All partial evil, universal good;
> And, spite of pride, in erring reason's spite,
> One truth is clear, Whatever is, is right.

In Hume's *Dialogues*, Demea tries the same tack, telling his companions,

> The world is but a point in comparison of the universe; this life but a moment in comparison of eternity. The present evil phenomena, therefore, are rectified in other regions, and in some future period of existence. And the eyes of men, being then opened to larger views of things, see the whole connection of general laws, and trace, with adoration, the benevolence and rectitude of the Deity through all the mazes and intricacies of his providence.

To which Philo replies by pointing out the asymmetry between pain and pleasure. Many people would prefer the absence of five minutes of agonizing pain to an hour of undiluted pleasure. But, more to the point, the illusion of pain is not what we expect from an omnipotent and wholly good creator.

The second tack is to deny the reality of God, as J. L. Mackie (1955) famously does in his article "Evil and Omnipotence." By supplementing Hume's argument with a couple of additional premises, Mackie argues that the existence of evil is incompatible with the existence of an omnipotent, omniscient, and perfectly good being. This quick victory for atheism was shortly reversed.

Theists made the logical point that, on the contrary, God and evil must be compatible, since the following set of propositions is perfectly consistent:

>(1) God exists.
>
>(2) Evil exists.
>
>(3) God has a morally sufficient reason for permitting evil.

Clearly, if (1) and (2) are consistent with (3), they must be consistent with each other. The defeat of the logical version of the problem of evil was an initial victory for theism and there was no need for atheists to deny it. As Rowe (1978) confessed, the logical version was untenable.

3. Is evil evidence against God?

But the battle wasn't over. Rowe (1979) and his allies fell back on the evidential form of the problem of evil: while the diversity and magnitude of evil in the universe is compatible with the God-hypothesis, evil by itself can still count as evidence against God and make it more reasonable to believe that there is no God than that there is. To illustrate this strategy by an analogy, suppose all we know is that Greg has the lowest marks in his class; this fact is compatible with his passing the class, once we later learn that nobody failed the class, but by itself, without other information at our disposal, it is evidence against Greg's passing and makes it more reasonable to believe that he failed.

Rowe took for granted that the basic form of evil is gratuitous or pointless suffering, whether it is suffering caused by natural disasters, like earthquakes and drought, or suffering caused by moral evils, like slavery and genocide. In the eighteenth century the famous example of natural evil was the Lisbon earthquake, but in the twentieth century it became the Holocaust, when the Nazi regime carried out the mass genocide of millions of men, women, and children on the basis of a trumped up ethnic mythology. (Anne Frank and her mother were included in that mass killing.)

Rather than turn to general examples of natural and moral evil, however, Rowe chose to focus on a particular case of what is, or appears to be, pointless suffering. Widely discussed in the literature, this came to be known as the Bambi case, in reference to the children's bedtime story, but with a very different ending. In Rowe's version, a fawn is trapped by a distant forest fire. Presumably, the fire was started by lightning, not arson or human negligence, so it is a clear example of a natural evil, and it causes the fawn to be horribly burned. Days later, after lingering in terrible pain, the fawn dies. Since, as far as we know, God could have prevented such suffering without losing a greater good or permitting an evil equally bad or worse, Rowe concludes that the fawn's suffering appears to be pointless. Even if it could be justified by some greater good, like improved forest management practices, it is only one of countless cases of such suffering, large and small, and it is unlikely that all of them could be justified by God-justifying reasons: i.e., some of them are *really pointless*.

That is the first step in Rowe's argument. It is of course a piece of inductive reasoning, and Rowe uses it to mount a full-scale deductive "argument for atheism based on evil." His argument can be simplified by using "God" in place of his more cumbersome expression "an omnipotent, omniscient, wholly good being," as follows:

1. There exist instances of intense suffering which God could have prevented without thereby losing some greater good or permitting some evil equally bad or worse.
2. God would prevent the occurrence of any intense suffering he could, unless he could not do so without thereby losing some greater good or permitting some evil equally bad or worse.

3. Therefore, God does not exist.

The argument is valid, so the question whether it is also *sound* depends on whether its premises are true. Rowe points out that, since the second premise is a necessary truth, expressing part of the meaning of "God", the crux of the argument is premise one, supported by the Bambi case. While he admits that the latter doesn't *prove* that premise one is true, he contends that it makes it *reasonable* to believe that it is true. Rowe might have added that probabilistic arguments are accepted every day in science and in practical life. After all, we can't prove that all humans are mortal, but on the basis of what we know about the past and human biology, it is exceedingly probable.

Rowe is aware that the theist can reject the first premise and thereby the conclusion. In fact, he later suggests that this move is the theist's best response. Using one or more of the traditional theistic arguments, or the appeal to religious experience, or the best explanatory hypothesis of phenomena , the theist can turn the argument upside down by arguing that, since God exists (the negation of the original conclusion), its first premise must be false (the negation of the original first premise). The question then becomes: which is more likely, on the basis of our *total* evidence, the existence of pointless suffering or the existence of God. On this point the theist and his opponent must agree to differ.

The atheist's argument is analogous to G. E. Moore's argument against radical skepticism:
    If the skeptic is right, I don't know that I have two hands;
    I do know that I have two hands;
    Therefore, the skeptic is wrong.

While Moore can't prove it without assuming the veridicality of perception, the assertion that he knows something seems more reasonable to accept than its denial. Or, to put it another way, Moore is taking for granted the possibility of knowing something, even if neither he nor anyone else can prove it. Though I concur with this point, it is liable to the difficulty that anyone can take refuge in that conception of knowledge, and so it is rarely philosophically decisive.

While Rowe's double-barreled argument implies that the theist is mistaken, he grants that theism is not necessarily irrational. The distinction between the truth and rationality of a belief is surely correct. Suppose you and I have different beliefs about the time because we don't have access to the same evidence. Knowing that the power has been off for an hour, I know that the clock on the wall is wrong, but, if you don't know about the power outage, you may be perfectly justified in believing that the time on the clock is correct, as it has always been reliable in the past (my example). In this case, my belief can be both true and rational, whereas your belief is false but nevertheless rational. I would have the same belief as you but for having access to additional evidence. Rowe uses this kind of distinction to explain what he means by "friendly atheism." The friendly atheist is one who believes that theism is false but not necessarily irrational. He may be compared to the unfriendly atheist, who believes that theism is both false and irrational, and the indifferent atheist, who believes that theism is false but has no opinion on its rationality, perhaps because he has never considered it as a separate question.

I believe that the concept of friendly atheism is interesting and useful, as it grants the theist something—his position is not necessarily irrational—and it is designed to allow the atheist to maintain the superiority of his position in point of truth. Nevertheless, it does raise a problem. What does the atheist know about suffering that the theist does not? It can't be the existence of pointless suffering, for as we will see, the theist has his own reasons for doubting the existence of such suffering. No doubt many cases of suffering *appear to* be pointless, but as many theists have pointed out, given human fallibility and the limits of human knowledge, there is a gap between appearance and reality, and atheists like Rowe have not closed that gap.

As Stephen Wykstra (1996: p. 126) says, "Looking around my garage and seeing no dog entitles me to conclude that none is present, but seeing no flea does not; and this is because fleas, unlike dogs, have low seeability; even if they are present, we cannot reasonably expect to see them in this way." In some cases the absence of evidence for something is evidence that something is absent, as in the case of a bomb threat that on investigation turns out to be a hoax, but in other cases the absence of evidence is another story. Until the microscope was invented, there was no direct evidence of forms of life too small to be seen with the naked eye, but it would have been rash to conclude that no such forms of life were possible. Similarly, we have no direct evidence of the existence of extra-terrestrial intelligent life, but would that be enough to justify us in believing that "we are alone in the universe"?

If the atheist cannot make good on his claim to know something about suffering that the theist does not, then it is hard to see how his position relative to the theist is like that between me and you in the clock situation. There it makes sense to say that, though both of us are rational, only one of us has a true belief, but it is paradoxical to contend that the theist and atheist are privy to the same information but only one of them has a true belief based on that information. For that to be possible, at least one of the parties must have misunderstood the original information or violated the equal information hypothesis by assuming that one of them has access to privileged information (Andre, 1985: p. 215).

The Bambi case for natural evil has been supplemented in two ways. First, the argument for pointless suffering can be extended to moral evil, as Bruce

Russell (1996) does. He cites a tragic case of actual evil in which a five-year-old girl was brutally beaten, raped, and strangled by one of the three men in her mother's household. We human beings can see no morally justifying reason for such a heinous act, but obviously it doesn't follow, from that fact, that there is no such reason. Perhaps God has a reason that is beyond our ken.

To explore this possibility, Russell explores three "Noseeum" principles, the third of which he finds acceptable: S's failure to see X is a reason to believe that X isn't there if and only if X's not being there is part of the best explanation of S's failure to see X (or is deducible from statements which are.) In Russell's view, the non-existence of God is part of such an explanation—though he doesn't put it that simply—so if there is no God, it follows that there is no God-justifying reason for the little girl's suffering. Surely, he is right *if there is no God*, but can we be sure of that the atheist is right? Russell is also right in suggesting that, if people were present who could intervene to prevent the crime against the child, they would be morally obligated to do so, but again the theist will insist that God may have grand purposes that go beyond immediate intervention. It is not clear, therefore, that the Sue case, as it has come to be called, adds much weight to the Bambi case.

The second supplement to the Bambi case was provided, ironically, by a well-known theist, Peter van Inwagen (2006). He devotes a chapter of *The Problem of Evil* to "The Suffering of Beasts." Beasts, of course, are nonhuman animals, and van Inwagen takes for granted that animal suffering has gone on for *millions* of years--suffering caused by predation and extinction events, whose scale dwarfs that of Bambi. Lacking free will of the human sort, this suffering cannot be justified by the popular free will defense, as can human suffering, so some theists have contended that animal suffering was due to the corruption of nature; as Plantinga says (1974: p. 58), "Something similar holds here; possibly natural evil is due to the free activity of nonhuman persons [e.g., Satan and his minions]" whose rebellion against God preceded that of man. Rather than accept this traditional view, van Inwagen proposes a different explanation. For him, God had a choice between creating a world like our own, with sentient animals capable of feeling pleasure and pain, and creating a massively irregular world, vastly different from our own. Since the latter world would have frustrated the divine purpose, God chose to create our kind of world. I mention this alternative not to support or attack it, but only to make the point that the problem of animal suffering, which goes deep into the prehuman past, is a headache for theists, quite apart from Rowe's fawn.

4. Plantinga and the case for theism

Despite the popularity of the Bambi case, many theists have challenged it and obliged Rowe to reframe his position in later articles, not as well known, but in the opinion of his critics, subject to the same difficulties and perhaps others. Rather than review that literature, I propose to look at an article by Plantinga (1996). While he has other works on the subject, in this one he targets Rowe's Bambi case, skewering it in a way that has encouraged other theists to pursue it avidly under the banner of skeptical theism. The general theme of skeptical theism is that human knowledge is very limited, especially of God and his purposes and doings. We may think we know that the universe originated in the big bang almost fourteen billion years ago, but we have no idea why or how the big bang began, if indeed it had a beginning. How come the entropy of the universe was so low at that point but has only increased since then and will eventually lead to the end of the physical universe as we know it today? We know that our bodies perish after death, but, as far as we know, isn't it possible that our spirit or soul will live on until the day of final judgment? Skeptical theists don't maintain that these things are so, only that they are possible. No one has proved that they are impossible. Nothing we know rules them out.

Plantinga invites us to consider the case of a child who dies a lingering and painful death from leukemia. Why couldn't God—an omnipotent, omniscient, wholly good *person (*Plantinga, 1983)—prevent that suffering for the child and her family, who may be good Christians? While he admits that his answer would not be suitable for pastoral care, Plantinga (p. 73) has no hesitation about the correct answer:

> True enough: we can't see what reason God, if there is such a person, has for permitting this child to suffer in that way. But (granted that it is indeed possible that he have a reason) can we just *see* that he doesn't have a reason? Perhaps his reason lies in some transaction involving free creatures of sorts we have little conception of. Perhaps God's reason involves a good for other creatures, a good for some other creature such that God can't achieve that good without permitting the evil in question. Or perhaps his reason involves a good for the sufferer, a good that lies in a future life.

Plantinga argues that the atheologian—his new word for the atheist—cannot justify the conclusion that there is no outweighing good for that child, without having to justify a whole flock of other propositions, such as "There is no afterlife." Since nobody has shown that there is no afterlife, Plantinga contends, nobody is in a position to insist on the absence of an outweighing good for the child. The atheologian is at fault, not for saying what is false, but for taking for granted what he is called upon to prove. The interesting question, I will argue, is whether Plantinga's own conclusions can escape a similar fate.

Plantinga (pp. 75-76) defines an evil as *inscrutable* if it is such that humans can't think of any reason why God would permit it to exist. But this means that practically nothing follows from the fact, if it is a fact, that some evil is inscrutable. As Plantinga observes,

Clearly, the crucial problem for this probabilistic argument from evil is just that nothing much follows from the fact that some evils are inscrutable; *if theism is true*, we would expect that there would be inscrutable evil. Indeed, a little reflection shows there is no reason to think we could so much as grasp God's plans here, even if he proposed to divulge them to us. But then the fact that there is inscrutable evil does not make it improbable that God exists. (My italics)

On examining, and finding fault with, three current conceptions of probability, Plantinga (p. 79) concludes that the atheologian is doomed to disappointment: none of them supports his claim that the existence of God is *improbable* or unlikely with respect to the existence of "10^{13} turps of evil (where the turp is the basic unit of evil)." As Plantinga (pp.86-87) rightly observes, people have very different reactions to encountering cases of appalling evil: it may strengthen their faith in God, weaken their faith, leave their faith unchanged but perplexed, or leave the faithless with the conviction that they are right.

Plantinga (pp. 87-88) also rightly notes that a proposition which is improbable relative to one piece of evidence may be probable relative to another. Knowing only that my new neighbor has a dog, I may infer that I will hear a lot more barking nearby, but on learning later that his dog belongs to a rare breed of dogs that don't bark, I will retract my previous induction (my example). That is the beauty of induction: it can lead to error but it can also be self-correcting. Plantinga grants that even if theism were inconsistent with evil, when it comes to the *total* evidence, not just the evidence of evil, the theist may have non-propositional evidence in the form of personal religious experience that renders belief in God probable, if not certain, *for him* on the basis of that experience. It may not do so for those who have never had such an experience, but that does not belie the evidence of his own experience. We should not make the mistake of thinking that *e* is evidence for *h* only if everybody, or nearly everybody, is familiar with *e*, like sense-experience.

Part of his argument is plausible. Since perfect pitch in music is an innate ability that a few people possess, but most do not, we cannot rule out the possibility that something like it may be found in the innate ability to receive religious visions or communications. Though I have no such ability, that gives me no reason to deny that Plantinga and others may have it. Though atheists commonly think of such persons as being deluded, Plantinga (p.91) says the shoe may be on the other foot. The theist may be inclined to think of the *atheist* as an unfortunate individual who suffers in his own way from a major spiritual defect, who cannot see what is open for more fortunate others to see. However, Plantinga does not address the well-known difference between the two cases. Perfect pitch can be tested by natural means, but the presence of special religious sensitivity seems to depend on self-reporting.

Plantinga is surely right to call attention to the limitations of atheism, but it is worth asking the comparative question "If atheism isn't subject to proof, isn't the same thing true of theism?" The atheist cannot *prove* that there is no *person* like God, no afterlife, no final judgment, and so on, but by the same token there is no proof of God, afterlife, day of judgment, and so on. Perhaps all of these things are possible, but what kind of possibility is this? Plantinga and others who follow him like to speak of "epistemic possibility," which seems to be akin to "logical possibility." For all we know about the world, certain unworldly states of affairs are not ruled out. For example, there is no contradiction in supposing that the body perishes at death but that the spirit or soul of the deceased continues to live on in some supernatural state. Equally, there is no contradiction in supposing that the body and "soul" perish at death. For that matter, we have no idea how to identify supernatural entities beyond the bare "possibility" of their existence.

The atheist need not be shaken by the epistemic possibility of life after death. Calling upon him to rule it out is asking him to do something impossible—namely, showing that the idea of surviving death is contradictory, like the idea of a square circle. It is like asking someone to prove a negative universal statement, like "There are no unicorns in the universe," instead of a restricted one, like "There are no unicorns on earth today" (meaning of course the live animal). So the inability to prove it shows nothing. We must be cautious about claims as to what is possible. It is epistemically possible that Sue is now enjoying life in heaven—nothing we know about the physical world rules it out—but atheists attach little weight to such possibilities. After all, they are epistemic possibilities, not probabilities. Nothing we *know* about the world and persons rules out the *possibility* of Sue's heavenly state, but it would be silly to treat that possibility as if it were a *live* possibility, like the possibility that you will spill your drink if you are careless or not be fit to drive if you drink too much. Asking the atheist to rule out remote possibilities isn't possible. And theists know it. That's why they ask the atheist to do it, counting on his failure to do it to support their position. Admittedly, the atheist can't prove that Sue's suffering is pointless, but the theist can't prove that it isn't either. It' a draw. Best to move on.

Since the free will defense is essential to the theist's position, Plantinga has no choice but to take it on. This is unfortunate, for neither philosophers nor scientists have been able to reach a consensus as to which of the two positions on free will—compatibilism or incompatibilism—is correct. As Samuel Johnson said of free will, "All experience is for it, all reason against it." According to compatibilists—sometimes called soft determinists because they believe that the feeling of freedom is compatible with determinism--you are free if you choose to do X and nothing prevents you from doing X, regardless of whether your choice was causally determined and could have been predicted by an omniscient being beforehand. You certainly aren't responsible for the genes you inherit at conception, so it's possible that you aren't responsible for anything that follows. As Schopenhauer said, "You are free to do what you will, but not free to determine what you will."

Incompatibilists, on the contrary, reject the idea that free will and determinism are compatible. That leaves open two possibilities: you can plump for determinism and the absence of real freedom—the position of hard determinism—or you can plump for real freedom and the falsity of determinism—the position of libertarianism. As I understand Plantinga and other theists who endorse the free will defense, they are libertarians. They reject determinism, at least as an explanation of human action, and also the concession that soft determinists are prepared to make for the sake of peace with determinism. (Modern physics, in any case, gives little support to universal determinism.)

To illustrate the libertarian position in a concrete way, as Plantinga does in his story of Curly, the mayor of Boston, suppose Curly is offered a bribe and has the opportunity to accept or reject it. We can represent his position in the form of two worlds, A and B, which are identical in all respects at time t when the bribe is offered (Hammond, 1956). At a later time $t1$, Curley accepts the bribe in world A, but what will his counterpart do in world B at that time? Will he accept or reject the bribe? If you are a determinist, there is no question but that he will accept the bribe in world B as well, for if two worlds are identical at one stage they will be identical at a later stage. But for a libertarian the outcome could be different. Yes, Curley could accept the bribe, but since he is free in the libertarian sense, he doesn't have to do so. He could reject the bribe—not necessarily for altruistic motives, but for self-concerned ones: he judges that accepting the bribe under present conditions is too risky. How can two persons identical in every respect come to make such divergent decisions at a later time?

Many people find the libertarian conception of free action unintelligible, since it seems to make free action comparable to tossing a coin.

Libertarianism seems to presuppose "the principle of alternate possibilities" (PAP): You aren't free in doing X unless you could have acted otherwise—i.e., done something else. While PAP has some intuitive appeal, Harry Frankfurt (1969) and others have shown that it is falsified by possible counterexamples. Suppose that Mary Reilly is a superscientist : she can anticipate how you plan to vote and even intervene if you don't plan to vote her way. Now you are about to vote on an important matter, but she is willing to leave the matter up to you, provided you vote as she prefers. If you do not, she is prepared to intervene and modify your vote so it accords with her wishes. In the end you decide to vote her way, so there is no need for her to intervene. In this scenario, you have acted freely, though in the nature of the case you could not have acted otherwise. (My example).

This of course is a science fiction case, but this kind of objection to PAP doesn't have to depend on science fiction. In the seventeenth century John Locke (1689) came up with a possible situation which will do as well. Suppose a guest at a drinking party drinks too much and passes out. For his guest's safety the host arranges for him to be taken to a bedroom and locked inside. During the night the guest awakens and is surprised to find himself in a strange room. He wonders whether to get up and leave the room, but, being comfortable, he decides to stay where he is. In doing so, he acts freely, but of course he couldn't have acted otherwise, for the exit is blocked. This example not only calls PAP into question, but conforms nicely to the compatibilist account of freedom. The sleeper is free, not because he could have acted otherwise, but because he did what he wanted to and nothing prevented him from doing so. Compatibilism, of course, is not the last word on the subject. But that is my point: the concept of free will has proved too contestable to bear the weight put on it by Plantinga and other theists.

5. Common sense and pointless suffering

As far as I can see, the theological case for or against pointless suffering remains open. While Rowe has been unable to close the gap between the appearance and the reality of pointless suffering, Plantinga has been unable to show that epistemic possibilities are live possibilities and, without making use of a controversial theory of free will, that there are God-justifying reasons for what appear to be cases of pointless suffering. Both philosophers proceed on the basis of understanding pointless suffering in grand metaphysical terms: it is suffering which God could not prevent without losing a greater good or permitting an evil equally bad or worse. But why must we proceed to tackle that problem in those terms? If your object is not to rule the possibility of God in or out, the question whether there is pointless suffering has a straightforward answer. Pointless suffering is suffering which is either (1) not deserved by the sufferer, because he or she has done nothing morally wrong, or (2) not necessary for the sufferer to gain some greater good not otherwise obtainable, because the greater goods in question are no more than "possible." Since there are many instances of suffering which are neither deserved nor necessary for some greater good, it is clear that there are many instances of pointless suffering.

But we need to be cautious. How can we tell whether someone does or does not deserve to suffer, or whether their suffering is of no future benefit to them or to others? There is more than one way of doing something morally wrong. We naturally think of wrong *actions* like lying or cheating or driving under the influence, or worse. But there are other ways of acting wrongly, like being negligent or careless or omitting to do something that is morally required. Perhaps you refused to help a needy person when you could easily have done so, or benefitted from being a member of a group that owes its privileged economic position to the oppression of minorities in past generations. It would be difficult to establish for any adult that they have never, on any occasion, done anything wrong in that expanded sense. Maybe that's why only young children are regarded as moral "innocents." Adults have lived longer and been more exposed to frustration and temptation, so it is unlikely that any of them has escaped the brush with some form of wrong-doing.

Even so, there are differences of proportion. Even if nobody is free of minor offenses, some people are struck by extraordinary disasters they have done nothing to deserve: the young woman raped by her teacher, the mother whose child is kidnapped and murdered when she can't pay the ransom, the elderly man robbed of his life savings at gunpoint, the window strangled in a home invasion, and so on. There are also cases where ordinary people find themselves in extraordinary situations, like war or revolution, where they may suffer injury and death for no other reason than being on the wrong side. None of these people may be moral innocents, but given the disproportionate level of suffering they undergo, they seem to be victims of pointless suffering.

Suffering can be regarded in a positive light, however. Speaking on behalf of the Irenaean theodicy, named after St. Irenaeus in the second century, John Hick (1994) proposes to regard suffering, not as punishment for sin, but as an opportunity for "soul-making." In creating man, God fashioned the body but not the soul of his creature. For that, something more was necessary: man had to engage with the problems of earthly existence and lift himself up by his own efforts. The earth was, in John Keats' words, "a vale of soul-making", in which struggle and suffering enable man to rise above the level of animals. As Hick (p. 179) says,

Men are not to be thought of on the analogy of animal pets, whose life is to be made as comfortable as possible, but rather on the analogy of human children, who are to grow to adulthood in an environment whose primary and overriding purpose is not immediate pleasure but the realizing of the most valuable potentialities of human personality.

This is a noble vision, giving suffering a positive role to play in human life but, as Hick admits, it accounts for a limited number of cases of suffering. And surely it is true that, just as suffering can lift up the human spirit, it can also crush it and leave nothing but devastation in its wake. In the school of hard knocks, perhaps only the fortunate few can pass the course of prescribed studies.

6. The reality of pointless suffering

Richard Swinburne (2004) proposes an epistemic principle he calls the "principle of credulity." The name is not flattering, for we commonly think of a credulous person as one who is easily taken in. Aside from the name, the principle is plausible. What it says in effect is that, if something appears to be the case, you are entitled to believe it, unless you have reason to suspect that it cannot be trusted. Though Swinburne uses it to support religious experience, it is less contentious to restrict it to more ordinary situations. For example, if you see drops of water on your window and wet patches on the ground, you are entitled to believe that it is raining, unless there is reason to think that your vision is defective or that the "rain" is produced by a sprinkler or broken water main. If your spouse tells you that she has a headache, you should believe her unless you have reason to think that she may be lying. By the same token, if you stub your toe and feel a jolt of crippling pain, you should believe that you are in pain, and it is hard to see how you could be mistaken. But should you believe that the pain is "pointless"? Well, presumably it was an accident, so in a sense it was pointless. But in another sense you could say that it is nature's way of telling you that something bad has happened to your foot and that you may need to treat it with special care. There is pain all right, but it isn't a clear example of pointless pain.

Take another case. Your friend by all accounts is a good woman. She has a loving family, many long-time friends, and is generous to all and sundry, but on a life-saving mission—to donate blood to save the lives of others--she is hit and severely injured by a hit and run driver. She ends up in severe pain in a hospital bed and, despite valiant efforts to save her, expires in terrible pain within a few days. You have no doubt that she suffered greatly, but was her suffering "pointless"? Well, you have no reason to regard it as deserved, as it might be if your friend had made a handsome living as a secret drug dealer, responsible for ruining the lives of many young people. Nor do you have any reason to believe that she is now better off, being in heaven and enjoying the reward of eternal bliss, for you have no reason to believe that hypothesis. Nor do you believe that other people are better off for her suffering.

No doubt some good might follow it. Perhaps she left a large sum on money in her will for a local orphanage, and they received those funds to do their good work. But you have no reason to believe that her suffering was necessary for that outcome. Had she died of natural causes a year later, the inheritance would have gone to the orphanage anyway. In short, you have every reason to believe that your friend's suffering was pointless.

The same thing of course goes for the stock examples of pointless suffering in the literature: the Lisbon earthquake, the Holocaust, and the Bambi and Sue cases. They are all striking examples of pointless suffering by any ordinary standard. We should not allow that fact to be obscured by the question whether God could have prevented them without losing a greater good or preventing an evil as bad or worse. It may be interesting for theologians to consider the implications of our ordinary beliefs about pointless suffering for the God hypothesis, but the outcome of their reflections should not lead us to think that the existence of pointless suffering is somehow controversial, when it is not. What is controversial, as Rowe and other atheists have argued, is whether the God hypothesis is true or at least reasonable to believe. Perhaps they have not succeeded in discounting that hypothesis, but whether they have or not, that is a separate question. It need not shake our ordinary convictions about the existence of pointless suffering. It is true that appearances can be deceiving, but we can't ignore the fact that if a pot on the stove is smoking, there is probably something in it that is burning. As Groucho Marx said, "If something seems absurd, don't be deceived, it probably is."

The question whether our ordinary beliefs about suffering are true or false is not unlike our ordinary beliefs about solid matter. Ordinarily we think of rocks and bricks as solid, whereas sponges and fishing nets are not. But according to physics, rocks and bricks are more like sponges than we naively think, for they are made up of large numbers of tiny atoms and are mostly empty space. Does that mean we should abandon the ordinary distinction between solid and porous matter? No, for there is a difference of scale. On the macroscopic scale of everyday life, where things can be seen as wholes, a rock is solid whereas a sponge is not. On a different scale, the nanoscopic scale of physics, where only a part of a whole can be seen, that part is not solid but porous and mostly empty space. Because of these differences in scale, a rock can be rightly viewed as both solid as a whole and as being made up of miniscule parts that are not solid. The two views are no more incompatible than the view that a distinguished orchestra can be made up of fine but not distinguished musicians or the view that a massive rain forest can be made up of individual trees that are small by comparison.

Similarly, suffering can be pointless for the sufferer and yet have a point for another party. Consider the myth of Sisyphus. The gods punish Sisyphus for tattling on them by sentencing him to a cruel fate: he must roll a heavy stone uphill only to have it come crashing down once it reaches the top, only to renew his labor with the same result, on and on, without end. We can presume that Sisyphus suffers from the prospect of his futile, endless labor, but we can also picture the gods gloating over their fiendish punishment. For them it has a point but it is still pointless for Sisyphus. Even if he deserves some punishment, does he deserve it for eternity? We need not suppose, then, that because suffering is pointless for the sufferer that it must be pointless, period. God may have a point in sending sinners to hell for eternity, but that doesn't mean that it has a point for them. On the contrary, their point in life may have been to avoid the prospect of hell.

It is true, of course, that suffering can have a point for someone, though they don't know it at the time. For example, a child may see no value in a painful injection, only to discover later in life that it spared her from a crippling disease. In short, we may have to wait to discover whether the suffering imposed is truly pointless. Theists often propose that we must wait until after death to discover the purpose of suffering, but, as atheists point out, such a claim takes for granted that such suffering has a purpose, and so it is question-begging. Pointless suffering remains a problem for the theist, and it can hardly be addressed by a story like the trials of Job. Job endures terrible tribulations but in the end he is said to be rewarded by gifts twice as good as anything he lost. True, the story shows no evidence of that expectation on his part, but if it ended with nothing but the suffering and natural death of Job, it would leave believers in doubt and dismay. Some readers are shocked when Robert Frost (1949, p.600) imagines God to confess, "I was only showing off to the Devil, Job,/As is set forth in chapters One and Two." Viewed in this light, Job's trials could be seen as another case of pointless suffering—pointless in the everyday meaning of the term.

I have no wish to deny that there are also cases where somebody considers their suffering, however agonizing and however undeserved or unnecessary, to have a point. This is possible because they believe, perhaps mistakenly, that their suffering contributes to the greater good, will be rewarded by heavenly bliss, or will allow them to rejoin loved ones in the afterlife. This is one of the ways in which human suffering differs from that of animals, for animals presumably have no such abstract beliefs. But if the greater good can be achieved without human affliction, if heaven is an illusion, or if there is no happy reunion after death, we have no option to regard such suffering as other than pointless. To claim that it might have a point for God strikes me as irrelevant.

Suffering, of course, is not the same as evil, for suffering in some cases can be justified. Bambi's suffering from her burns could be justified if it allowed her to recover and go on living a life suitable for her kind, and perhaps even Sue's beating and rape could be justified if it did not end in her death but allowed her to grow up and obtain some solace in later life for the experience, and use it to help young girls and women to avoid a similar plight. But by hypothesis we know none of these better outcomes are in play. It is hard to see how such suffering is other than pointless, for it was neither deserved nor necessary for something of greater value that could not otherwise be obtained. In short, the world would be better off without such suffering. It is no accident that cases of pointless suffering, real or imagined, give rise to the problem of evil.

7. Conclusion

Despite the efforts of theists like Leibniz and Plantinga, it is not only doubtful whether they can dispose of the problem, but whether it is even necessary to tackle the problem in traditional terms, as Hume and Rowe undertake to do. We can find pointless evil—a.k.a. pointless suffering—in our backyard, so to speak. We don't need to bring God into it, and doing so may distract us into pursuing irrelevant issues. The world may be better for some cases of suffering—people learn from their mistakes, criminals are locked up to protect the public, heroes risk their lives to save others—but it is worse for others—cases of extreme suffering that are undeserved and of no benefit to anyone. Perhaps humans can't have one without the other, but if so, that mixture of good and evil is, in the judgment of atheists, more telling for naturalism than for theism.

The main issue, as I see it, is to identify the typical causes of pointless suffering, whether it is physical pain or emotional distress, and to explain how human beings, individually or collectively, can best intervene to prevent or reduce future cases of such suffering. In practical terms, that means whatever we can do to prevent people from being treated as subhuman; whatever we can do to aid the victims of natural disasters; and whatever we can do to protect the young, the disabled, the frail elderly, and other dependents who cannot protect themselves. Needless to say, these are large tasks and it is doubtful whether theology will be useful or necessary to make progress with them. God, it is said, helps those who help themselves, so we cannot go wrong in undertaking to help ourselves.

References

[1] *A Masque of Reason*, 1949. In *Complete Poems of Robert Frost 1949*, New York: Henry Holt & Company.

[2] Andre, Shane, 1985. The Problem of Evil and the Paradox of Friendly Atheism, *International Journal for Philosophy of Religion*, Vol. 17, pp. 209-216.

[3] Andre, Shane, 1993. Was Hume an Atheist? *Hume Studies*, Vol. XIX, No. 1, pp. 141-165.

(4) Darwin, Charles. Letter to John Fordyce.

[5] Frankfurt, Harry, 1969. Alternate Possibilities and Moral Responsibility, *The Journal of Philosophy*, Vol. 66, pp. 829-839.

[6] Hammond, Albert, 1956. Adapted from his example, History of Philosophy class, McCoy College, Johns Hopkins University.

[7] Hick, John, 1994. Evil and Soul-Making. In Pojman, Louis P., ed., *Philosophy of Religion: An Anthology*, 2nd ed., Belmont, CA: Wadsworth Publishing Co., pp. 177-181.

[8] Hume, David, 1779. *Dialogues Concerning Natural Religion*, Book X.

[9] Locke, John, 1689. *An Essay Concerning Human Understanding*, Book Two, xxi, 10.

[10] Mackie, J. L., 1955. Evil and Omnipotence, *Mind*, Vol. LXIV, No. 254.
[11] Paley, William, 1802.. *Natural Theology, or Evidences of the Existence and Attributes of the Deity Collected from the Appearances of Nature.*

[12] Plantinga, Alvin, 1974. *God, Freedom, and Evil*, Grand Rapids, Mich., William B. Eerdmans Publishing Co.

[13] Plantinga, Alvin, 1983. Reason and Belief in God. In *Faith and Rationality*, Plantinga, Alvin & Wolterstorff, Nicholas, eds., Notre Dame: Notre Dame Press, pp. 16-93. Plantinga construes theistic belief, not just as belief in God, but as "the rationality of belief that G exists—that there *is* such a person as God," his italics, p. 18. Where traditionally God was conceived as a "being," Plantinga and van Inwagen have no hesitation in speaking of God as a person. In fact, van

Ingwagen attributes the first of God's ten intrinsic properties to his being "—a person. By a person, I mean a being who may be, in the most straightforward and literal sense, *addressed*—a being whom one may call 'thou.'" (See van Inwagen, Peter, *The Problem of Evil,* his italics, p. 20.) In addition, if God is powerful, knowing, and good, he has properties like those of human persons, except that, whereas they have them to a limited degree, he has them to a superlative degree. The problem with calling God a person, of course, is that he is immaterial and has no sex, whereas all the persons with whom we are familiar are material and have a sex. It is also unclear how a person without a body can act on material things or with propriety be referred to by the singular masculine pronouns "he, him, his."

[14] Plantinga, Alvin, 1996. Epistemic Probability and Evil. In Howard-Snyder, Daniel, ed. *The Evidential Argument from Evil*, Bloomington: Indiana University Press, pp. 69-96.

[15] Rowe, William L., 1978. *Philosophy of Religion: An Introduction.* Belmont, CA: Wadsworth Publishing Co.

[16] Rowe, William L., 1979. The Problem of Evil and Some Varieties of Atheism, *American Philosophical Quarterly*, Vol. 16, No. 4, pp. 335-341.

[17] Russell, Bruce, 1996. Why Doesn't God Intervene to Prevent Evil? In TheSecularWeb, originally published in *Philosophy: The Quest for Truth*, 3rd ed., Pojman, Louis P., ed., Belmont: Wadsworth, pp. 74-80.

[18] Sparrow, Carol Mason, 1947. Trans. *St. Augustine on Free Will,* University of Virginia Studies, The Dietz Press.

[19] Swinburne, Richard, 2004. *The Existence of God.* 2nd ed. Oxford: Clarendon Press.

[20] van Inwagen, Peter, 2006. *The Problem of Evil*, The Gifford Lectures Delivered in the University of St Andrews in 2003. Oxford: Clarendon Press.

[21] Wykstra, Stephen John, 1996. Rowe's Noseeum Arguments from Evil. In Howard-Snyder, Daniel, ed. *The Evidential Argument from Evil*. Bloomington: Indiana University Press, pp. 126-150.

SHANE ANDRE: BRIEF AUTOBIOGRAPHY

Shane Andre was born in Port Arthur—now Thunder Bay--Ontario, on Sept. 22, 1932, with the birth name "Conrad Eldredge Carlson," son of John Carlson and Laurie Menasce. Shortly after his birth, his mother left her husband, accusing him of cruelty, and moved to Montreal with her son. There she adopted the name "Lea Andre" and worked for a time as a fortune teller to support them. She read widely, joined the Theosophical Society, and encouraged her son to think for himself and do well at school. In 1945, at the end of the war, they moved to Vancouver, B.C., where Conrad, having completed grade seven, was encouraged by a numerologist to change his name officially to its present form.

In the heady days of the postwar boom, there were many changes in their personal lives. Shane spent a year in junior high, followed by a summer working long hours cleaning up in the galley of a coastal tour boat. In the middle of grade nine, he seized the rare opportunity to work his way on a cargo ship to Sydney, Australia, where he lived for several months. Meanwhile Lea entered her second marriage, which was not to last, and she fled to Whitehorse, Yukon for work. She spent her savings for Shane to fly back to Canada, where he rejoined her in June, 1946.

Summer and winter they shared a tent-cabin on the banks of the Yukon River in an area then known as "whiskey flats", but years later occupied by buildings of the territorial government. Shane got a summer job in the kitchen of the Whitehorse Inn and gradually moved up from cleaning pots and pans to preparing sandwiches and salads. He returned to school in the fall and did well in most subjects in grade ten, except for algebra and geometry, which at the time he thought were useless to him. Called upon to repeat those subjects, he refused to do so, despite his mother's pleas. By now he savored his growing financial independence. In a booming labor market, he could hire out as a cook, work full-time, and earn good wages—all this before he was twenty. At the time he saw no need to finish high school, let alone attend university.

In 1950, tired of the long, harsh winters in the north, Lea and Shane pooled their savings and bought an unfinished house and small acreage outside Kelowna---the center of a large, fruit-growing area in British Columbia. Both of them loved classical music and Lea encouraged Shane to pursue his newfound love of the piano. With her support he took piano lessons, practiced for hours daily, and even participated in a local music festival. Making rapid progress at first, he passed a set of exams for the Toronto Conservatory's Teaching Certificate and aspired to complete his studies at the Peabody Conservatory of Music in Baltimore, Maryland.

Shane lived in Baltimore from 1953 to 1958, supporting himself by working part-time. He completed the three-year Peabody Certificate in Piano Pedagogy, but by now, recognizing his limitations as a pianist and the dwindling opportunities for music teachers, he sought to broaden his academic background. To this end, he went to night school to make up missing high school work and eventually passed the G.E.D. at the 96% level. Then he took advantage of a joint program between Peabody and Johns Hopkins University to enroll in the Bachelor of Science program at McCoy College, Johns Hopkins University, which he completed *cum laude* in 1958.

Receiving a fellowship from Claremont Graduate School, Shane moved to Claremont, California, where he studied English and American literature, wrote a thesis "Maurice Morgann and Romantic Shakespearean Criticism," and completed the Master of Arts degree in 1959.

In the hope of getting a teaching job in Hawaii, he applied for a green card, but discovered that the market was closed to him as a non-U.S.-citizen. Happily, however, he was hired to teach grades three through eight in a one-room school on Canton Island--an atoll in the South Pacific near the equator, roughly halfway between Hawaii and Fiji. Despite the heat and humidity, he enjoyed the experience of working with students in different grades and of mixed ethnicities, and it was there that he first learned to drive a car. One special event over the Christmas holidays was Lea's arrival for a couple of weeks.

Shane's wanderlust next carried him to the American School in Guatemala City, Guatemala. It was a challenging assignment as he had to work with two groups of students--dependents of Americans working in the area and children of well-to-do local families, whose command of English was less developed. Hitherto Shane had taken two years of college level Spanish, but they failed to prepare him, he found, for fluent conversation in that language.

Though he was invited to remain at his post for another year, he was happy to leave, for another opportunity had come his way. Claremont Graduate School had opened a new Ph.D. program—this time in philosophy—and as an inducement to apply it offered more fellowships from the Intercollegiate Program of Graduate Study (colloquially known as "PIGS.") Though Shane at the time had little formal background in philosophy, he had always read widely in philosophy, in pursuit of the "big questions," and so he applied once again for a fellowship. To his surprise and delight he was accepted.

Returning to Claremont for the second time, Shane appreciated more fully his good fortune. Feeling that he had finally found his first love—the study of ideas—Shane was excited by philosophy in a new way, but realized that he had much to catch up. In addition, he loved the town of Claremont, with its old homes and gardens, mild winters, and leafy streets, where he could get around on a bicycle. Best of all, he had access to seminars taught by internationally recognized scholars, to the resources of several small liberal arts colleges associated with the Graduate School, and to an outstanding library. What was there not to like? Only the smog which occasionally blew in over the hills from Los Angeles, thirty miles to the west.

Shane remained at Claremont from 1961to 1964, supplementing his fellowship by working in the library and proctoring exams. Amongst the courses that most impressed him were the IPGS Seminar "Anatomy of Revolution," and seminars taught by Richard Popkin, Philip Merlin, Robert Fogelin, Morton Beckner, and E. J. Lemmon. Shane squeaked through the German-language exam with the aid of a dictionary and apparently was the only person to pass the Ph.D. qualifying exams in philosophy without having to retake any of its parts. He put this down, not to his superior knowledge, but to his acquired skill in hiding his ignorance.

When Shane left Claremont in 1964, he had completed all the requirements for the Ph.D. in Philosophy except for the dissertation. This ABD status qualified him for two junior teaching positions in the next two years, the first at San Diego State College, where he discovered for the first time how much he had to learn before he could teach others, and the second at Simon Fraser University-- a brand new university at the top of Burnaby Mountain outside Vancouver, B.C. Simon Fraser was on the trimester system and, on his first trimester off, Shane returned to Claremont to finish his dissertation, "The Verification Principle: Its Problems and Development," or die in the attempt. After months of preparation, working days and nights, Shane submitted the work to his committee, endured an oral exam in the presence of a visiting examiner, and could hardly believe his ears when Professor Fogelin greeted him with the words, "Congratulations, Dr. Andre." Sadly, the only person who died was the chair of his committee, E. J.

Lemmon--a brilliant English philosopher and logician, who had a heart attack the following summer while climbing the mountains outside Claremont.

Shane returned to Simon Fraser in 1966 and taught for another year, hoping to return to California. 1967 was memorable for two reasons. First, he met the woman who would consent to become his wife, Suzanne Olive McBennett, who was a sociology student at Simon Fraser. Second, he was able to return to California, having been offered a full-time position by the Department of Philosophy at California State College at Long Beach, later to become a University. While Long Beach was no Claremont, it had its advantages: he worked with a group of diverse but congenial colleagues, instructors were relatively free of external intrusion, students were unevenly prepared but sometimes very able, and, what would be increasingly rare later on, he was on the tenure track and could enjoy relative job security. That was important, for his son was born the following year. That helped to make up for the loss of his mother in 1969.

Though attaining his objective was hard work and exciting, the rest of Shane's philosophical career makes for conventional but dull reading, so it can be summarized briefly. Shane did receive tenure and was promoted by slow stages from Assistant to Associate to full Professor. Over the years he presented many papers to philosophy conferences both inside and outside CSULB, but his record of professional publications is brief if not skinny—articles in the *International Journal for Philosophy of Religion*, the *Canadian Journal of Philosophy*, the *Southern Review of Philosophy, Hume Studies,* and, after retirement, the *Open Journal of Philosophy*. He likes to think that, but for a heavy teaching load of lower division G.E. courses, he would have published more, but, as he admits, the truth is that he was probably lazy. Instead of using his summer breaks studying and responding to journal articles, he preferred to travel, though sometimes he taught summer school to earn extra money. On two occasions he was awarded

NEH Summer Fellowships to pursue philosophical projects, each of which led to a substantial publication. While his scholarly achievement was limited, he hopes he made up for it by his contribution to the education of hundreds, if not thousands, of students who passed through his classes. That is for others to judge.

Shane retired in 1994. Nevertheless, he never thought of retiring from philosophy, and, as an advocate of lifelong learning, he happily volunteered to teach philosophy classes to interested seniors for many years to come. In Long Beach he taught philosophy classes at Senior University (now Osher Lifelong Learning Institute) for about twenty years, and on Vancouver Island at Elder College for a dozen years or more. On the whole, they were rewarding years even without the pay, though they did impose a burden on Suzanne, who sometimes resented the time they took away from family life, as they did.

On the whole, Shane admits that he has had a good life, thanks to family, friends, travel, his untiring interest in philosophy, and his love of music. While he did not achieve as much as he had hoped, he has come to realize that this is a common, not a particular, failing. Though he complained about the limitations imposed by advancing age, he could think of no better way of summing up his life than with Robert Frost's wonderful metaphor, "I had a lover's quarrel with the world."

www.ingramcontent.com/pod-product-compliance
Lightning Source LLC
Chambersburg PA
CBHW061450300426
44114CB00014B/1924